D1365108

Making Sense of
Test-Based
Accountability
in Education

Laura S. Hamilton, Brian M. Stecher, Stephen P. Klein, editors

RAND
EDUCATION

Prepared for the National Science Foundation

The material in this book is based upon work supported by the National Science Foundation under Grant ESI-9978416.

Library of Congress Cataloging-in-Publication Data

Hamilton, Laura S.
  Making sense of test-based accountability in education / Laura S. Hamilton, Brian M. Stecher, Stephen P. Klein.
    p. cm.
  "MR-1554."
  Includes bibliographical references.
  ISBN 0-8330-3161-9
  1. Educational tests and measurements—United States. 2. Educational accountability—United States. I. Stecher, Brian M. II. Klein, Stephen P. III.Title.

  LB3051 .H3193 2002
  371.26'4—dc21

                                                              2002069685

RAND is a nonprofit institution that helps improve policy and decisionmaking through research and analysis. RAND® is a registered trademark. RAND's publications do not necessarily reflect the opinions or policies of its research sponsors.

Cover design by Eileen Delson La Russo

Published 2002 by RAND
1700 Main Street, P.O. Box 2138, Santa Monica, CA 90407-2138
1200 South Hayes Street, Arlington, VA 22202-5050
201 North Craig Street, Suite 202, Pittsburgh, PA 15213
RAND URL: http://www.rand.org/
To order RAND documents or to obtain additional information,
contact Distribution Services: Telephone: (310) 451-7002;
Fax: (310) 451-6915; Email: order@rand.org

Test-based accountability systems are based on the belief that public education can be improved through a simple strategy: require all students to take standardized achievement tests and attach high stakes to the tests in the form of rewards when test scores improve and sanctions when they do not.

Test-based accountability has achieved broad support as a strategy for improving public education. Standardized achievement tests have been used to measure students' educational progress for nearly a century, but the prevalence of tests, and the number of purposes they are being asked to serve, have grown substantially during the past two decades. In addition to the measurement function for which they were originally designed, large-scale achievement tests have become an essential component of efforts to reform education more broadly. Test-based accountability systems are in place in nearly every state, and advocates of these systems believe that the use of high-stakes tests will spur positive change in schools and classrooms.

But the emphasis on test-based accountability raises a number of important questions: Do these high-stakes tests measure student achievement accurately? How can policymakers and educators select the right tests, evaluate the test scores correctly, and attach the right consequences to the results of these tests to make accountability systems work as intended? What are the costs of developing and administering these tests? And what kinds of trade-offs do these policies introduce?

There is an extensive literature on the psychometric properties of achievement test scores and a much smaller, but still substantial, literature on the ways in which tests affect students, teachers, and other stakeholders in the education system. Yet for practitioners and policymakers who are responsible for making decisions about assessment and accountability systems, it is often difficult to find accurate and accessible information to inform these decisions. This book is intended to address that need.

With a grant from the National Science Foundation, RAND and other researchers have combined their knowledge to create this book, which should be of interest to practitioners, policymakers, and others who are involved in some way in test-based accountability systems but who are not technical experts in measurement. This book provides an overview of the major issues faced by those who develop, implement, and use test-based accountability systems, including a summary of the key technical considerations and a brief description of what is known about the impact of these systems.

This material is based upon work supported by the National Science Foundation. The research was carried out under the auspices of RAND Education. Any opinions, findings, conclusions, or recommendations expressed in this report are those of the authors and do not necessarily reflect the views of the National Science Foundation.

CONTENTS

FIGURES

TABLES

This book was written in response to school policymaking's growing emphasis on testing. During the 1990s, a number of states implemented educational accountability systems that assigned consequences for students, teachers, or schools on the basis of student test scores. The 2001 reauthorization of the Elementary and Secondary Education Act (the "No Child Left Behind [NCLB] Act of 2001") makes such test-based accountability a requirement for all 50 states. The goal of the law is ". . . to ensure that all children have a fair, equal, and significant opportunity to obtain a high-quality education and reach, at a minimum, proficiency on challenging state academic achievement standards and state academic assessments." The purpose of this book is to help educators and educational policymakers understand test-based accountability so they can use it effectively in the service of this goal.

States have considerable flexibility in developing their accountability systems, so long as those systems have at their core an appropriate feedback mechanism. Data on student achievement are collected annually and compared with a specific target. Failure to attain the target leads to successively harsher sanctions for schools, including ultimately reconstitution; success leads to recognition and financial rewards. When combined with greater flexibility from federal regulations and parental options to obtain supplemental educational services or move students from less-successful schools, these test-based incentives are supposed to lead to improvement for all schools.

The success or failure of these systems will depend, in part, on the specific choices states make when translating these general guidelines into practice and when refining their test-based accountability systems after they are operational. Yet, many educators and educational policymakers are largely untrained in test design and validation, and they are unfamiliar with recent research about test-based accountability systems. Greater knowledge about testing and accountability can lead to better system design and more-effective system management. It can also lead to more-effective use of test results for school planning, instructional improvement, and parental choice. Thus, in an era of test-based accountability, policymakers, educators at all levels of the system, and parents will benefit from becoming more "test wise."

To provide that understanding, and with the sponsorship of the National Science Foundation (NSF), we in RAND Education organized two conferences to share information about the state of the art in achievement testing, and then we developed this book. It is intended for educators, policymakers, and others who have an interest in educational reform, including

- state-level personnel who design and implement accountability systems, who determine the nature of and criteria for rewards and sanctions, and who are responsible for communicating information about the systems to educators and the public

- district personnel, school board members, and others who must interpret test scores and decide what actions to take

- teachers, principals, and other instructional leaders who must make decisions about how to respond to incentives and how to use data to change instructional practices.

This book is intended to help readers better understand these issues and make practical decisions about which tests to select and how to use the test scores. However, this is not the straightforward "how-to" guide one might wish for. Although test-based accountability has shown some compelling results, the issues are complex, the research is new and incomplete, and many of the claims that have received the most attention have proved to be premature and superficial. In fact, our goal is also to sound a gentle warning by highlighting the areas where caution is warranted, where getting results in one area requires trade-offs in another area, and where additional research is needed.

In *Making Sense of Test-Based Accountability in Education*, we discuss what policymakers and practitioners need to know in the following four key areas and conclude with guidelines for the design of effective test-based accountability systems:

1. How tests are used in test-based accountability systems

2. How to evaluate the technical quality of the tests and, therefore, the trustworthiness of the information they provide

3. How test-based accountability affects the practices of teachers and schools

4. How political considerations affect the policy debate.

UNDERSTANDING HOW THE TESTS ARE USED

A "test wise" educator or policymaker should understand something about the ways in which tests are used, particularly how they can be used in test-based accountability systems. For example, as explained in Chapter Two, standardized test scores are commonly reported in "norm-referenced" terms that indicate the relative standing of students with respect to a larger group. This type of score is familiar to many people, easy to interpret, and widely used in other areas of endeavor. However, in the context of accountability, where tests are used to determine student status with respect to specific content standards, "criterion-referenced" score reports may have more meaning. A criterion-referenced score indicates the degree to which a student has mastered a specific body of knowledge and is directly interpretable in these terms. Moreover, criterion-referenced scores can also be used to assign performance levels, such as "proficient" or "advanced," to help users interpret performance. The important thing to understand is that each reporting option has advantages and disadvantages, and the best option may be to report scores in multiple ways.

Chapter Two also explains many of the choices that confront developers of test-based accountability systems. These choices include the types of assessments used, the ways scores are aggregated, adjustments to scores to account for differences in student background, how test scores are combined in accountability indices, how performance goals are set, and how incentives are associated with student or school performance. Those responsible for designing test-based accountability systems face an array of choices along these dimensions, with each choice having its advantages and disadvantages. No single set of choices is best in every circumstance, and policymakers need to understand the trade-offs associated with each option.

EVALUATING THE QUALITY OF THE TESTS

A "test wise" educator needs to know how test quality is measured and what the trade-offs are among the different aspects of quality. Chapter Three provides a detailed discussion of the three criteria by which the technical quality of tests can be evaluated: reliability, validity, and fairness.

- *Reliability* refers to the degree to which a test's scores provide consistent information and are free from various types of chance effects. One way to think about reliability is to answer the question, What is the likelihood that a student's score, proficiency level, or pass/fail status would change if that student took the same test again the next day or took another version of the same test?

- *Validity* refers to the extent to which the scores on a test provide accurate information for the decisions that will be based on those scores. Validity investigations should synthesize evidence from a variety of sources and should be conducted with the test's intended purpose in mind.

- Appropriate interpretations of test scores also require that the test be *fair* to all examinees. That is, the test should produce the same score for two test-takers who are of the same proficiency level. Unrelated characteristics of the test-takers, such as gender, ethnicity, or physical disabilities, should not affect the scores they receive.

One of the key points to understand in evaluating and using tests is that tests should be evaluated relative to the purpose for which the scores are used. A test that is valid for one purpose is not necessarily valid for another.

A second key point is that test scores are not a definitive measure of student knowledge or skills. No single test score can be a perfectly dependable indicator of student performance, and there is widespread agreement among professional educators and measurement experts that high-stakes decisions about individuals should be based on factors other than test scores alone.

Finally, decisions about test design require trade-offs with respect to reliability, validity, fairness, and costs. For instance, longer tests are generally more reliable and can sample a wider range of content than shorter tests, but also impose more testing time on students. Test developers and users need to understand these trade-offs to make the best decisions when selecting and interpreting tests.

HOW THE SYSTEM AFFECTS TEACHING PRACTICES

A "test wise" educator must understand how test-based accountability affects educational practices. Chapter Four provides evidence about changes in behavior that have occurred as a result of high-stakes testing programs at the state level.

On the positive side, test-based accountability can lead to more instructional time, and educators working harder to cover more material in a given amount of time and working more effectively by adopting better curricula or more-effective teaching methods. These are the types of changes such systems were designed to promote.

However, test-based accountability can also lead to negative reallocation of instructional time to focus on tested aspects of the standards to the exclusion of untested aspects of the standards. It can lead to coaching students to perform better by focusing on aspects of the test that are incidental to the domain the test is intended to represent. Such narrowing of the curriculum has been widely reported in the research literature. At worst, test-based accountability can lead to cheating on tests, a practice that may become more common as the use of high-stakes testing increases.

Overall, the research suggests that large-scale high-stakes testing has been a relatively potent policy in terms of bringing about changes within schools and classrooms. Unfortunately, many of these changes appear to limit students' exposure to nontested curriculum, which clouds the meaning of the test scores. Understanding these influences can help policymakers and educators to design accountability systems with fewer negative consequences.

TAKING INTO ACCOUNT POLITICAL CONSIDERATIONS

A "test wise" educator should understand that testing policy represents a political solution to an educational problem. Chapter Five points out that the impetus for the movement toward test-based accountability comes from politicians, the business community, and others outside the education establishment. In fact, student testing has become a highly visible issue, characterized by the sort of politics that surrounds other high-profile issues.

Policymakers and educators are frequently at odds over testing policy. For example, policymakers often desire to use tests for multiple, high-stakes purposes, such as monitoring the status of the educational system, aiding instructional planning, motivating students to perform better, acting as a lever to change instructional content, holding schools and educators accountable, and certifying individual students as having attained specific levels of achievement. Policymakers often find themselves disagreeing with the professional standards of the testing and measurement community, which cautions against making high-stakes decisions on the basis of a single test, demands that tests be validated for each separate use, and calls for politicians to provide adequate resources for students to learn before holding students accountable.

It may be possible to reconcile good testing standards with political imperatives. Policymakers need to consider the full cost of the testing systems they seek to implement, including the need to provide every student who is subject to high-stakes testing with adequate and appropriate opportunities to learn the content of the tests. Policymakers need to persuade their constituents to be more patient in their judgments about public education. At the same time, they need to be more accepting of the limitations of tests and their potential uses. The testing and measurement community needs to provide policymakers with alternatives to current testing regimens that address the public's desire for schools that are more accountable, responsive, and effective. In the short term, measurement experts can identify changes that can be made to the existing tests and to the accountability systems to make them reasonably consistent with standards of good testing practice.

RECOMMENDATIONS FOR MORE-EFFECTIVE TEST-BASED ACCOUNTABILITY SYSTEMS

Finally, being "test wise" involves understanding the potential strengths and weaknesses of test-based accountability systems and being aware of some important features that will improve the usefulness of those systems. Chapter Six provides a number of initial recommendations for developing more-effective test-based accountability systems. These recommendations can serve as starting points for states as they address the challenges of the new regulations.

- Designers should recognize that accountability systems need not be static but can benefit from being dynamic and flexible. Test-based accountability systems should be monitored regularly to see how well they are performing, they should be evaluated periodically to assess their benefits and weaknesses, and they should be revised as needed to respond to problems and to benefit from insights gained in other contexts.

- Steps should be taken to maximize the technical quality of the system. For example, the system will be improved by incorporating multiple measures and multiple formats for critical decisions, by developing comprehensive student information systems that maintain individual-level data for analysis, and by using more-stable multiyear averages rather than single-year summaries as the basis for judging changes in achievement.

- Designers should attempt to maximize the positive effects of the accountability system on school and classroom practice while minimizing the negative effects. This goal can be promoted by conducting ongoing research to measure these effects, by providing appropriate professional development to make the purposes and mechanism of the system clear to those who participate in it, by designing the incentive system to focus attention on all students and reward gains at an appropriate level, and by attending carefully to the effects the system has on the educational opportunities provided to all students.

- Designers should also be cognizant of the political aspects of test-based accountability and take actions to incorporate the perspectives of all constituents. For example, they should make efforts to integrate the perspectives of politicians and educational measurement specialists, and they should attend to the needs of parents. Eventually test-based accountability will be held accountable itself in terms of its costs and benefits, and the educators who develop and manage these systems would be wise to gather as much information as they can on the cost and benefits of alternative educational reform options.

This book will help educators and policymakers make sense of test-based accountability. However, test-based accountability is a work in progress, and there will be additional technical, operational, and political challenges to overcome. Further insights will be developed as researchers, policymakers, and educators work together over the next few years to implement and improve these systems.

ACKNOWLEDGMENTS

We are grateful to the National Science Foundation for supporting this work and to Janice Earle, Maria Araceli Ruiz-Primo, and Larry Suter at NSF for the helpful feedback they provided along the way.

We benefited from our interactions with the many participants at the RAND/NSF Conference on Policy and Measurement Issues in Large-Scale Science and Mathematics Assessment, held in Washington, D.C., in March 2000. The presentations, demonstrations of current assessments, and thoughtful discussions among participants helped to shape this book. A special thank-you goes to Abby Robyn for her critical role in organizing this conference.

Our colleagues Tom Glennan of RAND, Joan Herman of the Center for Research on Evaluation, Standards and Student Testing at UCLA, and Sheila Barron of the University of Iowa reviewed two drafts of this book, and their comprehensive and constructive criticisms sharpened our analysis and informed our presentation.

Finally, we are indebted to RAND Research Communicator Shelley Wiseman for editing an earlier version of this report and improving the material, and our thanks to the RAND Publications Department team for their work on the editing, production, design, and marketing of this book.

Chapter One

INTRODUCTION

Laura S. Hamilton, Brian M. Stecher, and Stephen P. Klein

- How do we define terms such as *large-scale, high-stakes tests* and *test-based accountability systems?*
- Why is test-based accountability so popular?
- Why do policymakers and practitioners need to know more?

Standardized achievement tests have been used to measure students' educational progress for nearly a century, but the prevalence of those tests, and the number of purposes they are asked to serve, have grown substantially during the past two decades. Today, large-scale achievement testing is the linchpin of most state and national reform efforts and dozens of states have adopted formal accountability systems based on achievement test scores. Universal testing in reading and mathematics in the third through the eighth grades coupled with rewards and sanctions is the cornerstone of the ESEA (Elementary and Secondary Education Act) reform legislation passed by Congress in December 2001.

In the current environment, it is essential that educational policymakers and practitioners understand the strengths and weaknesses of large-scale tests—both as measurement instruments to judge student and school performance and as policy tools to change practice. Yet, most educators and educational policymakers are largely untrained in test design and validation, and they are unfamiliar with recent research about test-based accountability systems. For example, few understand the distinctions among different methods of estimating reliability, and fewer still know why this distinction may be important. Similarly, observers are often baffled by news accounts of the machinations surrounding accountability testing. Parents in one state sue to prevent the use of test scores for anything, while parents in another state sue to force the state to include their children in the testing program.

It seems clear to us that in the current climate, a basic understanding of testing gives educators and policymakers an important advantage. To provide that understanding, and with the sponsorship of the National Science Foundation (NSF), we at RAND organized two conferences to share information about the state of the art in achievement testing, and then we developed this book.

The purpose of this book is to explain the important issues in testing and accountability and provide policymakers some direction for improving the policies related to testing. In this introduction, we define our terms and elaborate on the reasons why an understanding of achievement tests and test-based accountability systems is critically important for today's policymakers and practitioners. In subsequent chapters, we provide some background about the use of tests in accountability systems, and we explore the technical aspects of assessment, the effects of tests on practice in schools and classrooms, and the politics of testing.

DEFINING THE TERMS

Large-scale tests are administered to large numbers of students across classrooms, schools, and districts. They are developed and mandated by parties external to a particular classroom or school. Large-scale tests include commercially developed tests that are administered as part of a district's or state's testing program, as well as tests that are developed by districts or states themselves.

Among the tests that are widely used today are the Stanford Achievement Test and the National Assessment of Educational Progress (see Chapter Two for more information on the tests). With the passage of the No Child Left Behind (NCLB) Act of 2001, we expect both wider use of the existing tests and a proliferation of alternative tests developed by school districts and private companies.

Tests have historically served an important measurement function, helping parents, students, teachers, and others to understand which students and schools were succeeding in which areas, and to identify students or schools that might need additional help. Tests have also been used, sometimes inappropriately, to determine what types of educational opportunities and services should be provided to which students.

Advocates of increased testing acknowledge the importance of these two measurement purposes, and they argue strongly that testing can also serve a third purpose—as a lever to influence instructional practice. They propose the following simple and direct strategy to achieve all three of these goals: Test all students in core academic subjects, reward schools and students who do well, and pressure those who do not. This strategy is implemented in the form of a *test-based accountability system*—that is, a set of policies and procedures that provide rewards and/or sanctions as a consequence of scores on large-scale achievement tests. The tests that are used for such purposes are often referred to as "high-stakes" tests, in contrast to "low-stakes" tests, which are used only to provide information on student performance (to teachers, policymakers, parents, or others). Thus, the terms *high-stakes testing* and *test-based accountability* are often used to refer to the same set of policies.

A test-based accountability system has the following four interrelated components:

- **Goals:** presented as a statement of desired individual or system performance

- **Measures:** quantitative indices of performance associated with the goals

- **Targets:** desired levels of attainment or improvement

- **Incentives:** identifiable consequences—positive or negative—based on the degree to which targets are attained.

Although different terms may be used, these are the basic elements in the current wave of accountability systems. Goals are usually stated in the form of curriculum or performance standards, leading to the term *standards-based reform*. Measures usually include standardized tests, which are selected or developed to be "aligned" with the goals or standards. The term *standardized* refers to tests that have standard tasks, administration conditions, and scoring rules. The term does not imply a particular test format, such as multiple-choice, or a particular type of score interpretation, such as norm-referenced.

Annual targets are defined in terms of a desired performance level for all students or a desired amount of improvement in performance. High-performing schools receive rewards, which might include public recognition, money to use for school improvement, or direct cash bonuses for staff. Consistently low-performing schools face various forms of intervention and possible reconstitution by state officials. Increasingly, individual students can also earn rewards, such as scholarship money, or they may face sanctions, such as retention in grade or denial of a high school diploma. Thus, for students, teachers, schools, districts, and states, the tests carry high stakes.

TESTS ARE USED WIDELY AND FOR SEVERAL PURPOSES

Large-scale testing is common throughout the K–12 education system. In fact, recent surveys conducted by Education Week (2001) and by the American Federation of Teachers (2001) indicated that all 50 states had testing programs in place in 2001. Nearly every public school student in the United States takes numerous large-scale tests during his or her K–12 career, and many students take multiple state and district tests each year. Currently, almost every state tests students in reading and math at one or more grade levels, and some also test in other areas, such as writing, social studies, and science.

Student testing has become more widespread as schools and districts have come to view test scores as useful for many different purposes. (The question of whether or not these purposes are appropriate and whether or not the tests satisfy them has not been settled, however.) For example, in one or more states or districts, achievement test scores are used to

- provide evidence of educational quality for public review

- provide information for teachers to help them improve instructional practices

- provide data for teachers, parents, and students to monitor student progress

- award cash bonuses to individual teachers, schools, and administrators

- determine which schools enter and exit from mandatory school-improvement programs

- allow parents to transfer students from their home school to another school

- make parents eligible for vouchers that can be used to pay for private schools

- determine the success of private companies that manage public schools

- evaluate the effectiveness of reform efforts or curriculum programs

- judge whether students should be promoted from one grade to the next

- place students into specialized educational programs (e.g., remedial, gifted, or bilingual classes)

- determine whether students will receive a high school diploma.

Clearly, scores on large-scale tests can have profound effects on the students who take them, and on the teachers and administrators who educate those students. As we discuss later in this introduction, test-based accountability systems are based on the assumption that using tests for some of these purposes is likely to lead to improvements in student learning.

NEW FEDERAL LEGISLATION MAKES TESTING MANDATORY

While most states already use tests now, all of the states will be reevaluating their assessment systems and making changes as necessary as a result of the new ESEA legislation.

The Elementary and Secondary Education Act (which is the authorizing legislation for the Title I compensatory education program) is the largest and most comprehensive K–12 federal education law. The Act, which was created in 1965 to provide educational assistance to disadvantaged children, contains more than 40 education programs. The most recent reauthorization of the Act occurred on January 8, 2002, when President Bush signed into law the NCLB Act. The reauthorization mandates annual reading and mathematics testing of students in grades three through eight. However, the legislation preserves much of the current variation among states in what tests are administered and how scores are reported and used.

The law is based on four basic principles: stronger accountability for results, increased flexibility and local control, expanded options for parents, and an emphasis on teaching methods that have been proven to work. Here are just a few of its provisions and requirements:

- Children in every state in grades three through eight will be tested every year in reading and math.

- Data from those annual assessments will be available to parents, citizens, educators, administrators, and policymakers in the form of annual report cards on school performance and on statewide progress.

- Statewide reports will include performance data disaggregated according to race, gender, and other criteria not only to demonstrate how well students are achieving overall but also to report the schools' progress in closing the achievement gap between disadvantaged students and other groups of students.

- The Act will allow the creation of up to 150 local flexibility demonstration projects for school districts interested in being able to consolidate all funds they receive from several programs in exchange for entering into an agreement holding them accountable for higher academic performance.

- A sample of students in each state will participate in the fourth- and eighth-grade National Assessment of Educational Progress (NAEP) in reading and math every other year in order to help the

U.S. Department of Education verify the results of statewide assessments.

* All limited English proficient (LEP) students will be tested for reading and language arts in English after they have attended school in the United States for three consecutive years.

THE RATIONALE FOR TEST-BASED ACCOUNTABILITY SYSTEMS IS COMPELLING

The rationale for test-based accountability systems is compelling to many policymakers and observers. For example, the National Alliance of Business recently published a report that urged increased pressure for schools to perform at higher levels than they do now:

> . . . It is increasingly clear to business leaders, however, that the public education system will not respond to such calls for reform in the absence of pressure to do so. . . . In public schools, educators and students have faced few consequences for their failures and even fewer rewards for their successes. The National Alliance of Business believes that introducing such consequences and rewards into public education is essential to raising student achievement and spurring schools to continually improve (National Alliance of Business, 2000, 1).

As this excerpt illustrates, one of the fundamental assumptions underlying test-based accountability is that the information and incentives that are built into these systems are not only beneficial but necessary for ensuring that school personnel commit themselves to the goal of improving student achievement. Views on the specific reasons for this assumption vary. Some advocates argue that test-based accountability is important primarily for the information it provides—test scores inform teachers about which students are performing well and which need extra help, thereby enabling teachers to adjust their instruction appropriately. Others claim that the use of rewards and sanctions is critical for motivating teachers and principals to focus their efforts on instruction in core academic subjects. Without such incentives, they claim, school staff become distracted from this central goal. Although views on the specific means by which incentives improve instruction vary, the opinion that these types of incentives are necessary is widespread and has influenced policy at the local, state, and national levels.

Proponents of test-based accountability argue that this approach has been effective, citing evidence from states that have implemented such systems and have subsequently seen their test scores rise. For example, recent studies in Florida, North Carolina, and Texas suggest that schools in the lowest category on the state's performance scale (and therefore subject to sanctions) tend to show more improvement than those in the second-to-lowest category (Carnoy, 2001). Thus, it appears that accountability systems are having the desired effect, particularly on the lowest-performing schools.[1] Furthermore, although its absolute cost is not inconsequential, testing is less expensive than many other reforms, particularly those that seek to change classroom practices through direct intervention (Linn, 2000). Its relative cost makes it attractive to educators and policymakers seeking to change public education.

Partly as a result of such arguments and evidence, state and federal policymakers have come to regard test-based accountability as the most promising approach for improving education. Support for test-based accountability has been growing throughout the past decade among other key groups as well, including parents. Although there have been some recent reports of a "testing backlash," most surveys of parents reveal strong support for the use of tests in evaluating schools and students (Business Roundtable, 2001a). Lawmakers in both major political parties have advocated for increased accountability, typically with the backing of most of their constituents. This broad support makes it highly likely that test-based accountability in some form is here to stay.

---

[1] As we discuss in later chapters, there are a number of alternative explanations for the rapid test-score gains observed in many states and districts. One plausible explanation is that the gains result from an influx of resources and support to low-performing schools, but existing data make it difficult to separate any resource effect from other influences.

TEST-BASED ACCOUNTABILITY COMMANDS
SUBSTANTIAL RESOURCES

As we noted in the previous section, test-based accountability is relatively inexpensive compared with the total cost of education and the cost of large-scale classroom interventions. The research evidence does not provide definitive information about the actual costs of testing but the information that is available suggests that expenditures for testing have grown in recent years. Achieve, Inc., for example, recently estimated that total spending on testing among the 50 states increased from $165 million in 1996 to a projected $330 million in 2000 (Achieve, Inc., 1999). Testing costs include expenditures for designing, constructing, piloting, revising, distributing, and scoring tests, as well as analyzing and reporting results. They also include the costs associated with other components of the system, such as program administration and financial rewards given to schools. In any case, the cost of a formal accountability system is small relative to other expenditures but is large enough to command the attention of policymakers and call for careful decisionmaking.

Other costs imposed by test-based accountability systems are difficult to estimate. These include the value of the class time that is required for administering tests as well as the class time consumed by test-preparation activities. The General Accounting Office (1993) included class time in its estimate of the total cost of achievement testing in the states in 1990 to 1991. Its estimate was $516 million, figuring that the average amount of time spent in direct testing and related activities was seven hours per student. The estimate does not include time for more-extensive test preparation activities.

There are also costs associated with changes in school and classroom practices that occur as a result of testing. The evidence is clear that testing and accountability lead teachers to reallocate their time away from some instructional activities and toward others (see Chapter Four). If this reallocation lowers student achievement in subjects such as history or science, it may be considered a cost. Advocates of accountability often argue that this reallocation is actually beneficial because it means that teacher time is spent on the "important" content and skills.

Whether these changes represent a net benefit or loss is unclear at present. In fact, how these changes add up may differ for individual students. Consider the elementary school teacher who reduces science instruction to provide more basic-skills instruction in mathematics. For some students, particularly those students whose mathematics proficiency is low, more math instruction provides a critical foundation for future learning. For other students, the reallocation may result in increased boredom and reduced motivation as a result of their spending less time on a favorite subject, and may therefore represent a net loss. There may even be costs borne by families, such as the costs of test-preparation materials or services that parents may feel pressured to obtain. This pressure is likely to become greater as a result of the increased use of test scores to determine graduation or grade promotion.

Existing research does not provide evidence about the "right" amount to spend on testing, for example, and it doesn't answer the question of whether the money spent on testing and accountability would be more likely to lead to improved achievement if it were spent on other efforts instead, such as raising teacher salaries or reducing class sizes. If more testing yields a noticeable improvement in achievement, the costs may be judged as acceptable.

ABOUT THIS BOOK

This book is intended primarily for educators, policymakers, and others who have an interest in educational reform and who need information to help them understand and make decisions about the current test-based accountability systems. The intended audience includes

- state-level personnel who design and implement accountability systems, who determine the nature and criteria for rewards and sanctions, and who are responsible for communicating information about the systems to educators and the public

- district personnel, school board members, and others who must interpret test scores and decide on what actions to take

- teachers, principals, and other instructional leaders who must make decisions about how to respond to incentives and how to use data to change instructional practices.

Some information in this report will be more useful to some groups than to others. For example, the discussion in Chapter Three on how to evaluate technical information on tests is probably most relevant to those who are responsible for making decisions about which tests to use.

At the same time, we believe that anyone affected by test-based accountability systems should be broadly informed about the issues addressed in this book. For example, although teachers and principals are usually not asked to decide what kind of reliability evidence to obtain before a test is adopted, an understanding of what the reliability information means (provided in Chapter Three) may help them make better decisions about how to use test-score data for school and classroom improvement.

The book focuses on large-scale, high-stakes tests used in accountability systems for K–12 schools and students. We do not address other large-scale tests, such as those used for college admissions or professional licensing. Although many of the same technical considerations are applicable to these tests, the specific context of K–12 accountability drives our presentation of technical and policy issues.

Chapters Two through Six address four key policy questions:

- How prevalent is large-scale high-stakes testing and how do current test-based accountability policies vary across states?

- How should the trustworthiness of information produced by high-stakes tests be evaluated?

- How does test-based accountability affect the practices of teachers and schools?

- How do political considerations affect the use of tests?

We attempt to provide a straightforward summary of what is currently known about these issues, so that efforts to design, implement, monitor, and improve accountability systems will be informed by existing evidence.

The chapters in this book are organized as follows:

- Chapter Two provides a discussion of the role of tests in accountability systems, including a brief history of large-scale testing, the relationships between standards and tests, and the different methods of reporting test results.

- Chapter Three summarizes the technical criteria for evaluating large-scale tests, focusing on validity, reliability, and fairness.

- Chapter Four reviews the consequences of high-stakes testing on school policies and classroom practices, in particular on the behaviors of principals, teachers, and students.

- Chapter Five looks at testing in a political context.

- Finally, Chapter Six outlines our recommendations for improving test-based accountability systems.

Chapter Two

TESTS AND THEIR USE IN TEST-BASED ACCOUNTABILITY SYSTEMS

Laura S. Hamilton and Daniel M. Koretz

- What is the history of testing and accountability in America?

- How do today's tests and accountability systems differ from those in the past?

- What are the features of the tests that vary from state to state?

Although current test-based accountability systems are often presented as novel and innovative, they have roots in the policies of past decades, and they represent a mix of new and long-standing approaches. Some of the most pressing issues raised by the current systems arose in earlier programs as well.

In this chapter, we provide a short history of large-scale testing and test-based accountability.[1] We then describe features of the accountability systems and tests that are in place today. We describe several ways in which state testing systems vary. We discuss content and performance standards, which in today's systems typically serve as the means for communicating a common set of goals. Following that, we present information on the features of tests. We then discuss several other issues related to large-scale testing, including methods of

---

[1] Sections of the introduction to this chapter are reprinted and adapted from the following source, with permission of the publisher: Koretz, D. (1992). State and national assessment. In M. C. Alkin (ed.). Encyclopedia of Educational Research, 6th ed., 1262–1267, Washington, D.C.: American Educational Research Association.

reporting, procedures for setting performance targets, and test-based rewards and sanctions. Broadly speaking, these categories represent key components in the process of implementing a test-based accountability system: Standards are established, leading to the selection or development of tests in the relevant subjects. Tests are then administered and scored, and results are reported. A target is established, and rewards and sanctions are distributed as a function of whether schools or students meet the specified target.

This chapter is intended to be primarily descriptive, and we do not advocate a specific approach for any of the topic areas we discuss. Instead, the discussions are intended to illustrate the range of options that may be considered when new tests and accountability policies are put into place and to alert readers to some of the potential problems and trade-offs associated with some of these options. (Chapter Six includes additional discussion of some of the issues raised here and provides some guidance for those who need to make decisions about which of these features to implement.)

A BRIEF HISTORY OF RECENT TRENDS IN LARGE-SCALE ASSESSMENT

Large-scale external testing—that is, assessments using tests developed externally to the schools in which they are administered—dates back to the 19th century in American education but initially was not widespread. By the latter half of the century, such tests were used for a variety of purposes, including monitoring the effectiveness of instructional programs and comparing schools and even teachers (Resnick, 1982). The first standardized achievement test battery, the Stanford Achievement Test, was originally published in 1923 (Resnick, 1982), and the role of standardized testing grew markedly over the following years (Haney, 1981). It has been a fixture of elementary and secondary education ever since. Figure 2.1 illustrates the major developments in the history of testing.

Nonetheless, large-scale testing between World War II and the 1960s was fundamentally unlike current programs in several respects. During that period, the primary functions of large-scale testing were to assess individual students and to evaluate curricula (Goslin, 1963; Goslin, Epstein, and Hallock, 1965). Tests were not commonly used

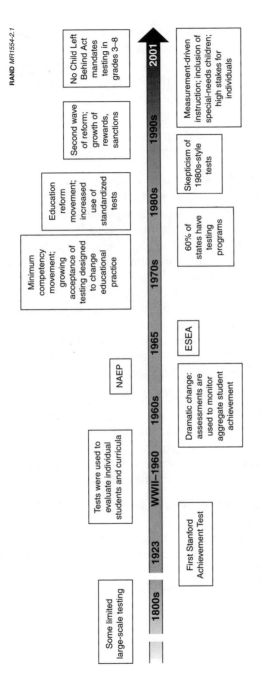

RAND MR1554-2.1

Figure 2.1—Brief History of Testing and Test-Based Accountability

to monitor educational systems or hold schools accountable for student performance, as they are now, and with a few exceptions (in particular, college admissions tests and tests used to determine placement), the consequences of scores for teachers and students were minor.

Using Assessments to Monitor Aggregate Academic Achievement

The transformation of the functions of large-scale testing programs began in the 1960s. The establishment of the National Assessment of Educational Progress (NAEP), a recurring assessment of a nationally representative sample of youth, was a major step in using assessments to monitor aggregate academic achievement, even though for many years NAEP did not provide information about performance at the level of individual states. Another major step was enactment of the Elementary and Secondary Education Act (ESEA), which established the federal Title I compensatory education program and required that the program be evaluated. Standardized achievement tests became a central means of evaluating Title I programs. Some observers (e.g., Airasian, 1987; Roeber, 1988) viewed this as a key step toward the use of tests as monitoring and accountability devices.

Despite these changes, most states still lacked statewide testing programs at the end of the 1960s. Statewide programs rapidly became more common after that; by the end of the 1970s, roughly 60 percent of the states had statewide testing programs, most of which were mandatory, and by 1990, most did (Koretz, 1992). Currently, all states but two (Nebraska and Iowa) administer uniform statewide exams.

This growth in state-mandated testing resulted in part from the rapid spread of minimum-competency testing programs beginning in the early 1970s (Jaeger, 1982). These programs required that students pass a basic-skills test, most often as a requirement for graduation (*exit testing*) but in some instances as a requirement for promotion between grades (*promotional-gates testing*).

Evolving from Minimum-Competency Testing to Measurement-Driven Instruction

Although the minimum-competency testing movement began to recede within a short time, it marked a lasting transformation in the functions of large-scale testing. It made the great majority of students, and by extension their teachers, accountable for performance on these tests. More fundamentally, it changed the link between test scores and educational improvement.

One could argue that before the minimum-competency testing movement, the primary function of most large-scale testing was to provide information about performance, and tests were designed with this goal in mind. Tests were often used with the expectation that this information would lead to educational improvement, but educational change was not a primary function guiding the design of testing programs. Minimum-competency testing, however, was accompanied by a growing acceptance of the notion of "measurement-driven instruction" (Popham et al., 1985), that is, the idea that testing programs could be designed specifically to generate changes in educational practice. Measurement-driven instruction remains a cornerstone of assessment policies today.

The Education Reform Movement and Increased Use of Standardized Tests

The minimum-competency testing movement was rapidly followed by the "education reform movement" of the 1980s. The early part of that decade saw an upsurge of concern about perceived weaknesses of the U.S. educational system. Debate about the decline in aggregate test scores that had begun in the mid-1960s intensified, even though scores had begun to rebound (see Koretz, 1986). Reports from NAEP showed that many students were failing to master even rudimentary skills, and several studies showed that American students compared unfavorably to their peers in other nations. This period saw the publication of numerous influential reports calling for reforms, most notably *A Nation at Risk* (National Commission on Excellence in Education, 1983).

These concerns sparked a nationwide education reform movement, one of the most consistent elements of which was an increased use of standardized tests. For example, Pipho (1985) noted that "Nearly every large education reform effort of the past few years has either mandated a new form of testing or expanded uses of existing testing." Existing testing programs were broadened, and tests were made more difficult. Most of the testing of the 1980s relied on multiple-choice tests, although some systems included other types of testing as well, in particular, direct assessments of writing.

The new wave of testing was generally used for accountability, and results were often tied to serious consequences for students or educators. In addition to exit and promotional-gates testing, states began to experiment with financial incentives and the threat of state intervention in schools or districts performing poorly on the tests (National Governors' Association, 1989).

The Second Wave of Reform: Testing Higher-Order Skills

By the end of the 1980s, however, skepticism about the testing initiatives of the 1980s was becoming widespread. Critics pointed to evidence of two negative effects: degraded instruction, as some teachers focused on various undesirable forms of test preparation and inappropriate teaching to the test rather than enriched instruction, and inflated test scores, that is, increases in scores that did not signify a commensurate improvement in achievement. Growing acceptance of this criticism was one impetus for a change in testing during the 1990s that some observers called the "second wave of education reform."

The second wave of education reform retained confidence in measurement-driven instruction. The establishment of formal rewards and sanctions for educators based on test scores continued to grow. Both financial rewards for improved scores and sanctions for poor performance, such as state intervention or reconstitution of schools, were implemented in numerous states across the nation.

The new reforms, however, called for major changes in the assessment programs used for accountability. The weaknesses of the assessment programs of the 1970s and 1980s were attributed by many observers to the forms of testing used, and many reformers therefore called for using types of assessment that would, they hoped, circumvent those problems. In particular, reformers called for "tests worth teaching to"—that is, tests designed in such a way that, if most instruction was targeted at helping students do well on the tests, the students would still be receiving high-quality instruction. In addition, policymakers in many states wanted assessments to focus on so-called higher-order thinking skills. The resulting changes in assessment generally entailed reliance on formats other than multiple-choice questions, including portfolios of student work, hands-on standardized performance assessments, essays, short-answer questions, and hybrid tasks that entailed both group and individual work. Concurrent with these changes in testing was the nationwide effort to create new state-level content and performance standards, and the new assessments were often presented as implementing these new standards.

While the focus on measurement-driven instruction continues to be a centerpiece of education policy, the nature of large-scale assessments and accountability systems has continued to evolve since the onset of the second wave of education reform in the early 1990s. The recent changes have been of six types:

- New efforts at both the federal and state level to include students with special needs (those with disabilities or limited proficiency in English) in the large-scale assessments used for the general student population

- In response to statutory requirements, ongoing efforts to integrate Title I accountability testing into general statewide assessment programs

- In some states, increasing specificity of the content and performance standards undergirding large-scale assessments

- A shift in some jurisdictions back toward more reliance on traditional (i.e., multiple-choice) forms of assessment

- A movement in some jurisdictions away from survey assessments (those that cover a broad content area such as mathematics) and milepost testing (testing a subject at only a few grade levels, such as 4, 8, and 11) and toward curriculum-based assessments (tests that assess the objectives of particular courses, such as geometry)

- A resurgence of high stakes attached to the test results for individual students.

The reinstitution of high stakes for individual students has paralleled the minimum-competency testing movement in that exit testing is more common than promotional-gates testing. The current form of high-stakes testing differs from minimum-competency testing, however, in numerous respects, including the difficulty of many of the performance standards students must meet, the inclusiveness of the testing requirement, and in many states and districts, the coupling of high stakes for students with high stakes for educators (sometimes labeled "balanced" or "symmetric" incentives).

HOW LARGE-SCALE TESTS ARE USED TODAY

As discussed in Chapter One, although current accountability systems in education take various forms, they all share a number of features:

- **Goals** that indicate desired content and performance standards
- **Measures** of progress toward those goals, including tests and reporting strategies
- **Targets** for performance; e.g., status and change measures
- **Incentives,** such as rewards or sanctions, based on the attainment of the targets.

Most states have some form of a test-based accountability system in place that incorporates these features, and policymakers have periodically discussed the merits of a national system that would serve a similar purpose. The No Child Left Behind (NCLB) Act of 2001, which reauthorized the Elementary and Secondary Education Act of 1965, mandates some specific components of a test-based accountability system, such as annual reading and mathematics testing of students in grades three through eight, the use of tests aligned with standards, specific forms of reporting, and the imposition of an accountability system that tracks annual changes in school performance. Nonetheless, substantial variation among states in the nature of testing programs is likely to persist.

Content and Performance Standards

Like earlier versions of ESEA legislation, the NCLB legislation emphasizes the need for assessments that are tied to clear and rigorous content and performance standards. Most state accountability systems, as well as some districts, share this emphasis. For example, as stated in the NCLB Act of 2001, the new law calls for

> Challenging academic content standards in academic subjects that specify what children are expected to know and be able to do; contain coherent and rigorous content; and encourage the teaching of advanced skills; and challenging academic achievement standards that are aligned with the State's academic content standards; describe two levels of high achievement (proficient and advanced) that determine how well children are mastering the material in the State academic content standards; and describe a third level of achievement (basic) to provide complete information about the progress of the lower-achieving children toward mastering the proficient and advanced levels of achievement.

This language from the NCLB act is similar to that included in earlier versions of the ESEA. It refers to two broad classes of standards: academic content standards and academic achievement standards. The latter are often called *performance standards.* The Council of Chief State School Officers (CCSSO) published a handbook to assist states in setting standards consistent with 1994 federal legislation (Hansche, 1998). The handbook defines content and performance standards as follows:

> Content standards answer the question, What should students know and be able to do? They are descriptions of the knowledge and skills expected of students at certain grade levels.

> A system of performance standards includes (1) performance levels, labels for levels of achievement; (2) performance descriptors, descriptions of student performance at each level; (3) exemplars, illustrative student work for each level; and (4) cut scores, score points on a variety of assessments that differentiate between performance levels (Hansche, 1998, 12 and 14).

Both content and performance standards play important roles in the process of communicating goals and expectations, and it is therefore critical that the process of developing standards be informed by input from representatives of all relevant stakeholders. However, a discussion of how to develop standards is beyond the scope of this report. For clear and useful advice on this topic, we refer readers to the CCSSO handbook mentioned earlier.

In the remainder of this section, we discuss two topics that are critical to understanding how tests are used in a standards-based system: norm-referenced and criterion-referenced score interpretations and alignment between tests and standards. Use of test-score information in a standards-based system requires that performance be reported based on what students have accomplished rather than where they rank among their peers. It also requires that assessments accurately reflect what is communicated by the standards; in other words, that standards and tests be well aligned.

Norm-Referenced Score Reporting

Although some observers use the term "norm-referenced" incorrectly to refer to the type or content of tests, the term properly refers solely to the manner in which scores are reported. *Norm-referenced reporting* involves describing the performance of an individual unit (which can be a single student or an aggregate, such as a school, district, state, or even an entire nation) in terms of its position in a distribution of scores of other units. The most common examples are tests that report the performance of students in terms of a distribution of scores, using metrics such as national percentile ranks or normal curve equivalents (NCEs).[2] The major commercial achievement tests provide reporting of this sort, placing the performance of each student on the distribution of performance in national samples. Table 2.1 lists some examples of scores that are often provided by commercial testing companies.

---

[2] NCEs and T-scores (see Table 2.1) are described here as a form of "standard scores." In some applications, they are actually "normalized scores," which means the original distribution of scores was converted to create a normal or bell-shaped distribution. This distinction is unimportant for most applications.

Table 2.1

Types of Norm-Referenced Scores

Percentile rank (PR)	Indicates the percentage of a reference group (often, the national population of students) who obtained lower scores than a given student. Thus, a student with a national percentile rank (NPR) of 75 scored higher than 75 percent of a national sample of students.
Standard score	Expresses a student's performance in terms of how far the student's test score is from the mean. The scores are transformed to have a specific mean and standard deviation (or SD—a measure of the spread of scores). Examples are z-scores (mean=0, SD=1) T-scores (mean=50, SD=10), and normal curve equivalents (or NCEs—mean=50, standard deviation=21.06). (See Footnote 2.) Thus, a student with a T-score of 60 is one standard deviation above the mean, which is roughly a PR of 84.
Grade equivalent (GE)	Expresses a student's performance in terms of the grade level at which that performance would be typical. GEs are generally expressed in decimal form, such as 5.7, in which the first number is the grade and the second is the month (for ten academic months, with zero representing the performance of students first entering that grade level). A student who scores a 5.7 on a fourth-grade test has the same level of performance as would a median student in the seventh month of fifth grade if that student took the same test. GEs are a *developmental scale* designed to examine growth. In any subject and at any level, the median increase in performance over a year of growth is 1.0 GE.

Test results may be reported in terms of a variety of norms. For example, users of the Iowa Tests of Basic Skills can obtain normative reports that compare the performance of students to those of other students in large cities, students in Catholic and private schools, students in schools in low- or high-socioeconomic areas, and students in international schools. Users may also obtain reports using school norms that compare the average performance of individual schools to the distribution of school averages, which are much less variable than the distribution of students' scores (Hoover et al., 1994). Some of the results of NAEP are reported in terms of state norms—that is, states are compared with each other in terms of average scores, various percentiles, and the percentages of students reaching each of the performance standards, which are called "Achievement Levels" in

NAEP reports. The results of the Third International Mathematics and Science Study (TIMSS) are also primarily presented in terms of country norms—that is, the performance of each country is reported in terms of a distribution of country means. Although neither of these tests is designed to support the kinds of norm-referenced interpretations that are common with many commercial tests, many of the results are nonetheless typically reported in a normative way.

Criterion-Referenced Score Reporting

The principal alternatives to norm-referenced test score reporting are *criterion-referenced reporting* and *standards-based reporting*. Technically, criterion-referenced tests report performance in terms of the degree of mastery of a specific criterion, which could be a specified range of content. In practice, however, the term "criterion-referenced" is generally used to refer to a test that reports performance relative to one or more fixed *levels* of performance, such as minimum-competency tests. The term "standards-based" reporting is typically used in the same way. *Standards* refers to both the material students are expected to master (content standards) and the fixed levels of performance they are expected to reach (performance standards). Neither standards-based nor criterion-referenced reporting requires any comparison among students or other units.

The growth in standards-based accountability has led to increasing use of this form of reporting, which many educators and policymakers believe is necessary for conveying information about whether students have met the standards and for providing clear learning goals for students and teachers. California provides an example of a state that has supplemented its norm-referenced reporting with additional measures designed to convey information about students' progress toward achieving state-developed standards. In the case of California, performance on criterion-referenced tests is reported using five categories: Advanced, Proficient, Basic, Below Basic, or Far Below Basic. The state established the Proficient level as the goal for all students. Some states, such as Massachusetts, have assessment programs that provide only standards-based information in certain grades.

The method of reporting has implications for the design of a test. For example, a test that is intended to support criterion-referenced interpretations should reflect a specific content framework or set of standards so that performance can be interpreted in terms of what students know and can do. In theory, neither the difficulty of test items nor the items' ability to differentiate among high-performing and low-performing students is necessarily important; if all students show mastery, then that is what the test should reveal. In contrast, if a test is designed to differentiate among higher-performing and lower-performing students, it is important that the items show a reasonable range of difficulty, are not too difficult or too easy, and show some degree of differentiation among higher- and lower-performing students.

Comparing the Two Types of Score Reporting

In practice, however, the design of norm-referenced and standards-based tests is often not as different as the considerations that we present here suggest.

Most standards-based assessments (including all of those mandated by the recent reauthorization of ESEA) report performance at more than one level, and typically at three levels. Using multiple levels requires that the tests include items with a considerable range of difficulty. Moreover, the developers of standards-based tests must address item difficulty when the tests are used for high-stakes decisions because the range of item difficulty will affect the reliability of scores.

Conversely, the design of norm-referenced achievement tests starts with the consideration of content. Typically, an examination of curricula and textbooks is used to create a matrix of content and skills common to many curricula. This matrix is loosely analogous to the content standards that underlie current standards-based tests. Items are then written to map to that matrix. Statistical considerations are used to choose among those items; for example, items that map well to the matrix but are too difficult for most test-takers to answer will generally be avoided. However, items that meet statistical criteria and differentiate among higher- and lower-achieving students would *not* be retained if they did not map to the matrix of desired content and skills.

In fact, some tests are used for both norm-referenced and standards-based reporting. NAEP provides an interesting example. Originally,

NAEP was designed simply to describe the performance of American youth. It included neither performance standards nor a formal set of norms. In the 1980s, however, the assessment was redesigned. In the process, it developed some of the characteristics of a norm-referenced test, such as a developmental scale, but it still did not include norms such as national percentile ranks. In recent years, NAEP has accrued additional functions, and it is now reported in both norm-referenced and standards-referenced forms. For example, the performance of a participating state is reported in terms of both a ranking of states (that is, state norms) and the percentage of students reaching each of three performance levels (the NAEP Achievement Levels, which are labeled Basic, Proficient, and Advanced).

In one sense, the recent evolution of NAEP, in particular the establishment of the achievement levels and their growing prominence, has made the assessment more standards-based. But the standards have also been used for normative reporting, perhaps indicating both a desire for comparative information and the utility of norm-referenced reporting for making sense of performance. The performance of states and other groups is reported in terms of the percentages of students reaching each standard (among other ways of reporting performance), but states are then ranked in terms of these percentages.

Although norm-referenced reporting is sometimes criticized as not providing information about what students have actually accomplished, its continuing use in state, national, and international assessments reflects its usefulness. Norm-referenced reporting is familiar and easily understood, and users turn to normative data to interpret a wide range of performance information. For example, the score a college applicant receives on the SAT I or American College Test (ACT) college-admissions test is norm-referenced; even if the student pays no attention to the percentiles supplied with the scale scores, the student will know whether his or her score is a relatively good one by comparing it with the scores of other applicants, by long-standing expectations of the school that is considering the applicant, and by the admissions records of colleges. Few college applicants need to be told that a combined SAT I score of 1500 is very good or that a combined score of 900 is weak, even though few if any would be able to describe the level of mastery (that is, the performance criterion or standard) corresponding to a given score. Similarly, the great attention paid to the "horse-race" aspects of state NAEP comparisons and the results of TIMSS indicates the usefulness of normative reporting, even though many of the users of those results do not realize that those results are norm-referenced.

Normative information is also commonly used in interpreting a wide range of performance information other than that provided by achievement tests. For example, when a Washington, D.C.–area high school student recently ran a mile in just under four minutes, people took note for normative reasons: Runners that fast are rare, and no high school runner had ever before run a mile that quickly. Another example comes from the use of growth charts that provide information on typical height and weight for children of various ages. Most parents are familiar with these charts. Understanding where a child ranks at several points in time enables parents and pediatricians to evaluate whether the child is progressing at a slower or faster rate than other children.

Nonetheless, norm-referenced reporting does not directly inform the user about the test-taker's mastery of important knowledge or skills. For that reason among others, many states have placed primary emphasis on standards-based systems in which they report the percentages of students who reach one of several predetermined performance standards. This form of reporting entails difficult decisions about how many performance levels should be created, what method should be used to set those levels, how high they should be set, and what they should be called.

Disadvantages to Reporting Performance Solely as Norm or Criterion Referenced

Although the use of performance levels is intended to provide information about examinee proficiency that is clearer than what is available via norm-referenced reporting, there are some disadvantages to reporting performance solely in standards-referenced or criterion-referenced form:

- First, regardless of the method used to establish standards, the choice of cut points is fundamentally judgmental and is often called into question. There are a number of approaches to standard setting, many of which are considered defensible if carried out properly, but all share a reliance on expert judgment.[3] Users of test-score data are often unaware that the determination of what scores constitute "proficient" or "advanced" performance might change if the panel had been constituted differently or had been given different instructions for setting the standards.

- Second, the use of levels or cut scores reduces the amount of information that is conveyed relative to other types of scores because it fails to distinguish among scores that fall within a particular category, no matter how far apart those scores are. In other words, there is no distinction between the student whose performance is slightly above the cut score and one whose performance is far above it. As a result, many changes in performance will go unrecognized. Consider two schools, each of which improves student performance by 20 test-score points over the course of a year. If one school starts with students who are just below the cut score and moves them above the cut score, whereas the other starts with students whose performance is far below the cut score and whose later performance is just slightly below it, interpretation in terms of the cut score will reveal improvement at the first school but not at the second. In the context of high-stakes accountability systems, the use of performance levels or cut scores may create incentives for educators to focus their efforts on improving the achievement of students whose performance is close to the cut score and to ignore those whose scores are far above or below it.

These examples illustrate that all of the methods of reporting have both advantages and disadvantages. For this reason, it is often beneficial to report results in several forms. For example, reporting performance in terms of several different performance standards lessens (but does not eliminate) some of the disadvantages of standards-based reporting. Alternatively, standards-based reports can be paired with reporting that is based on a continuous scale. Using a norm-referenced scale, such as percentile ranks or GEs, as the continuous

---

[3] A discussion of procedures for standard setting is beyond the scope of this report. Interested readers should see Hambleton (1998) for an overview of current methods and Hambleton et al. (1998) for a discussion of procedures used with performance assessments.

scale offsets some of the limitations of each kind of scale and provides information for parents, students, and teachers who want to know what content and skills students have mastered and how they are doing compared with other students.

ALIGNING TESTS AND STANDARDS

For a standards-based accountability system to work properly, there must be some assurance that the tests that are used are aligned with the standards. In other words, the content and level of difficulty of the test items must reflect what is communicated by the standards. Alignment between tests and standards is in fact an explicit requirement of the Title I legislation, both the recently adopted version and the earlier ones.

As of 2001, 12 states had contracted with an outside organization to conduct a review of alignment between tests and standards (Education Week, 2001). The early results indicate that there is much work to be done: Of the ten states whose standards and assessments were examined by Achieve, Inc., only one, Massachusetts, was judged as having developed "strongly aligned standards and tests" (Achieve, Inc., 2002, 33).

However, what alignment means operationally is unclear, and a wide variety of assessments can be developed to link to a single set of standards. Alignment is typically evaluated by content-area experts who examine the test items and standards and evaluate whether they appear to be capturing the same content knowledge or skills. One factor that sometimes makes this evaluation difficult is the lack of specificity in many published standards. Many states have been criticized for promulgating standards that are vaguely worded and difficult to interpret. Analyses conducted annually by the American Federation of Teachers (AFT) suggest this problem has diminished: 29 states were classified by the AFT as having English, mathematics, science, and social studies standards that were "clear and specific" in 2001, compared with 22 states in 1999 and only 13 states six years ago (American Federation of Teachers, 2001). Standards that do not clearly convey what is expected at each grade level make it difficult for teachers, administrators, parents, and students to gear their efforts toward meeting those standards and increase the risk that educators will focus too intently on the specific content of tests to ascertain what should be emphasized in instruction.

Alignment between standards and assessments can also be limited by considerations of cost. The expense associated with developing a new assessment, combined with a desire for norm-referenced information, have led many states to use commercially available tests in their assessment programs, either with or without adaptation. In addition, states do not always test in all of the subjects for which they have developed standards, and research shows that teachers tend to pay more attention to tested subjects than those that are not tested, regardless of whether there are published standards for those subjects (see Chapter Four for a further discussion).

One of the rationales for using standards to guide test development is that the standards approach will improve the utility of tests as instructional tools. Some of the difficulties associated with using standards to guide instruction are highlighted in a recent report by the Commission on Instructionally Supportive Assessment (2001), a group convened by several teachers' and administrators' organizations to produce a guide for policymakers implementing test-based accountability systems. The commission of experts in instruction, curriculum, and assessment published a set of nine requirements for state-mandated tests. These requirements are intended to promote the use of tests that improve the quality of instruction children receive. For example, the commission suggests that states prioritize their content standards, create tests that focus on a relatively small number of high-priority standards, and produce individual student-level scores for each of these standards. This would undoubtedly improve the value of test-score information for teachers, parents, and students alike.

As the commission acknowledges, however, implementation of these recommendations may lead to narrowed instruction that focuses only on the small number of standards included in the test. To circumvent this problem, the commission suggests that states offer classroom-based assessments of standards that are not addressed by the formal accountability system and that states monitor the curriculum to ensure that inappropriate narrowing does not occur. These are useful suggestions, but neither of them is likely to address the problem entirely. Without incentives to improve performance in areas that are included in the standards but not on the test, the class-room-based assessments are unlikely to have a significant impact on instruction. And there are currently few known cost-effective approaches for gathering valid data on curriculum and instruction at the classroom level.

This lack of clear solutions to the problem of aligning tests and standards illustrates the continuing tension between the need for accountability system developers to communicate clear goals to educators and the risks of narrowing instruction. It is also important for developers and users of these systems to resist the temptation to make a given set of assessments serve multiple purposes.

As we discuss later in this book, tests that produce reasonably valid information for one purpose may not be valid for another. It is natural for educators and others who are concerned about the amount of instructional time being devoted to testing to want the tests to be useful for instructional purposes. However, the kinds of tests used for large-scale assessments typically cover a broad range of content and are not tailored to a specific curriculum, and the necessity of scoring large numbers of tests means that results are often not available until several months after test administration. As Linn (2001, 3) points out, such tests "are more suitable for providing global information about achievement than they are the kind of detailed information that is required for diagnostic purposes." Therefore, developers of accountability systems must carefully weigh the competing objectives of large-scale measurement and instructional improvement, and must be wary of claims that any one set of measures will adequately and fully address both concerns.

Types of Assessments

An examination of statewide assessment programs across the United States reveals great diversity in the types of assessments used and the contexts surrounding their administration. Recent surveys conducted by Education Week and by the American Federation of Teachers indicated that all 50 states had testing programs in place in 2001, although several midwestern states continue to permit a large amount of local district latitude in standard-setting and reporting (Education Week, 2001; American Federation of Teachers, 2001). In particular, Nebraska and Iowa require districts to report student achievement but allow the districts to choose the test. In this section, we discuss several of the key variables that distinguish state testing programs—subjects and grade levels tested, use of commercially developed versus state-developed tests, and test format.

Subjects and Grade Levels Tested. Although every state has an assessment program in place, the subjects and grade levels tested vary widely. In 2001, 28 states had or were planning tests in each of the four core subjects of reading, mathematics, science, and social studies in at least one grade in all three levels—elementary, middle, and high school (American Federation of Teachers, 2001). In many states, English and mathematics are tested more frequently than are science and social studies. For example, students in Mississippi and California take reading and math tests in nearly every grade in elementary and middle school, but do not take a science or social studies test until they are in high school (American Federation of Teachers, 2001).

Because the NCLB Act emphasizes reading and mathematics testing, it is likely that many states will continue to test primarily in those subjects. This introduces yet another trade-off: Focusing testing in this manner underscores the particular importance of reading and mathematics and makes the testing program more manageable, but it creates the risk of some undesirable curriculum reallocation effects, which are discussed in Chapter Four.

Commercial Versus State-Developed Assessments. Some states use commercially available standardized tests whereas others develop their own assessments or hire contractors to do so. Here again, each choice has its advantages and disadvantages. Commercial tests are generally of high quality, with extensive pre-testing of items, and they provide national norms against which to compare students' performance. However, many states do not consider the available tests to be well aligned with their own standards. In response, many states that use commercial tests either pair them with state-specific tests or augment them with additional items that are intended to reflect the state's standards. These additional items are, in some cases, developed by the same publishers that provide the original tests and may be drawn from the same item pool as the original items.

California's Standardized Testing and Reporting program (STAR) provides one example of this approach. In spring 2001, California administered the Stanford 9 test to students in grades 2 through 11 for the fourth consecutive year, allowing the state to track growth in scores and to compare their students' performance with that of the Stanford 9's national norming group. Because the Stanford 9 was not originally designed to measure California's standards, there was a need to supplement it with other measures. The California Standards Tests were added to the program and were scheduled to be included in the state's formal accountability system in 2002. In 2001, for example, fourth-grade and seventh-grade students also took a 60-minute open-ended writing test. Although some critics of the program have expressed concern over the increased testing time required to accommodate these tests, others view the addition of the California Standards Tests and the writing test as a positive development that is likely to lead to better instruction on previously neglected skills and topics. California plans to reduce emphasis on the original Stanford 9 over time and instead focus on the newer Standards Tests. For states that need to adopt new tests quickly to comply with NCLB, the practice of supplementing commercial tests with state-specific items or test forms may provide an approach to designing a program that can be implemented rapidly but that is aligned with state standards.

Test Formats. States also vary in the formats of the tests they administer. All 48 states with uniform statewide assessment programs include multiple-choice items, partly because of the low costs and generally high reliability of such exams. In recent years, the majority of states administered short-answer items in at least some grades and most also used extended-response (e.g., essay) items to test writing in English. The use of extended-response items in subjects other than English has been relatively rare; in 2001, only seven states administered such items. Two of these (Kentucky and Vermont) included portfolios of student work (Education Week, 2001).

Formats other than multiple-choice are generally costly, in large part because they are almost always scored by people rather than machines. Other formats also typically consume more testing time and they can generate a number of technical problems, such as lower reliability per unit time and greater difficulty in equating test forms.[4] Nonetheless, many educators and policymakers consider these disadvantages to be offset by other attributes of non-multiple-choice formats. For example, many educators believe that open-response formats are better able than multiple-choice tests to measure problem solving and higher-order thinking skills and that open-response tests are necessary to ensure alignment with state standards.

Another justification for using tests with formats other than multiple choice, as discussed earlier in this chapter, is the belief that they are "worth teaching to"—that is, the use of such tests should, in theory, reduce the likelihood that teachers will respond to high-stakes testing by emphasizing discrete facts and should encourage teachers and students to focus more closely on sophisticated forms of reasoning and knowledge. There is some evidence that this has happened in at least some states that have implemented non-multiple-choice formats (see Chapter 4). This creates yet another trade-off among the choices facing states: Multiple-choice items are less expensive than many other formats (and, as discussed in Chapter Three, generally more reliable) but may not capture the range of skills and knowledge addressed by the state's standards.

Reporting the Results of Large-Scale Assessments

Effective test-based accountability requires accurate and accessible reporting of assessment results. The type of reporting influences both the usefulness of the information to stakeholders and the incentives that the accountability system creates. One critical reporting decision is the choice between norm-referenced versus criterion-referenced interpretations, discussed earlier in this chapter. In this section, we discuss three additional reporting-related issues: the unit of reporting (e.g., individual or school), the use of adjustments for student or school background characteristics, and the process of creating an index for accountability purposes.

Individual Versus Aggregate Reporting. An important reporting decision involves the unit of reporting. Teachers and parents typically

---

[4]Several systems for computer scoring of essays have been developed, but none is currently used in a statewide testing program.

receive scores for individual students. For other reporting purposes, however, scores are generally aggregated to the level of the class-room, school, district, or, as in the case of NAEP, the entire state or nation.

Decisions about unit of reporting have implications for the design of assessments. For example, an advantage of reporting only aggregate scores is that matrix sampling of items is possible. *Matrix sampling* involves administering different sets of items to different students to enable larger coverage of a domain than is possible when all students must take the same test. This makes the results of the test a better indicator of mastery of the curriculum, and it makes inappropriate narrowing of instruction more difficult. However, matrix sampling has its disadvantages as well. Foremost among them is that it makes it very difficult (and often impossible) to provide valid scores for in-dividual students because the scores from the various forms of the test are not comparable. Therefore, the recent trend toward in-creased student-level accountability, as is evident in the increased use of high school exit exams, makes it difficult for states to use ma-trix sampling.

One state that has used matrix sampling is Maryland. Its Maryland School Performance Assessment Program (MSPAP), which is being administered for the last time in spring 2002, included tests in several academic subjects administered to students in grades three, five, and eight. Because the tests consisted of performance-based tasks that require more administration time than do multiple-choice items, matrix sampling allowed a fairly broad range of content to be as-sessed in a relatively brief testing time. However, although the state computed individual-level scores for students, testing experts warned that those scores were not sufficiently reliable or valid for the purposes of reporting to parents or others (Hambleton et al., 2000), and in most cases those scores were given to families only upon re-quest.

Although this testing system has served some purposes well in Maryland to date, Maryland and other states that have used matrix sampling in the past have abandoned it because of demands by poli-cymakers and others for student-level scores. At least one state (Massachusetts) uses matrix sampling but uses only common items (those administered to all students) as the basis of scores for students; both common and matrix items are used to report results for schools and districts. The matrix-sampled items are included for the purpose of trying the items out to understand how they function and to determine whether they should be included as common items in subsequent years. This approach is useful as a means of cycling new items into the assessment but offers none of the other advantages of matrix sampling.

Some states, as well as the NCLB legislation, require that performance be reported separately for groups of particular interest to policymakers, such as minority students and students with disabilities. This type of reporting is generally referred to as *disaggregated reporting*.[5] Some accountability systems go a step further, holding schools accountable for raising scores among all groups for which disaggregated scores are reported. Although such policies are usually intended to ensure that schools attend to the instructional needs of all students, the requirement that schools meet separate targets for each group may actually result in disproportionate failure rates among diverse schools. There is some measurement error associated with each computation (see Chapter Three), and the more targets that are set, the greater the chance that a school will fail to achieve one or more of them simply because of random error. (Kane, Staiger, and Geppert [2001] provide a more technical discussion of this problem.)

It is also important to keep in mind that the degree of accuracy is influenced by the level of aggregation. School-level scores typically display greater degrees of accuracy than do individual-level scores, although in some cases, such as when there is significant student mobility at a school, school-level information may be misleading. Decisions about whether to report school-level, classroom-level, or student-level scores, and whether to disaggregate for specific groups, should be informed by the purposes for which scores will be used and the desire on the part of stakeholders for specific types of information. However, as the earlier discussion of matrix sampling

---

[5]Use of the term "disaggregated" in this context may be confusing because the resulting reports are aggregated from individual students to groups of students. The term "disaggregated" refers to breaking apart the scores of a larger unit of aggregation, such as a school.

indicates, these decisions are also affected in large part by cost and feasibility.

Adjusting for Student Background. In some testing contexts, reported scores are adjusted for school and student characteristics. There is a strong relationship between student achievement and socioeconomic status and other aspects of student background. Therefore, schools that serve certain types of students, such as poor children, tend to face lower achievement levels at the time of entry than do schools that serve children from more advantaged families. Some policymakers and educators have argued that test scores should be adjusted to take these differences into consideration. The principal argument in favor of adjusting is that it is fairer in the sense that schools are compared with others that have more-similar populations. Schools with disadvantaged populations, for example, are not compared directly with schools with highly advantaged populations.

The principal contrary argument to using adjusted scores is that they have the effect of institutionalizing different standards for different students. An additional complication is the generally poor measurement of student background characteristics in school databases, which makes most adjustments inadequate. For example, poverty is typically measured using the percentage of students participating in the free or reduced-price lunch program, but this is a very coarse indicator that masks extensive variation in income and wealth. Yet another problem with adjusting scores for background characteristics is that the quality of education may be correlated with these characteristics—for example, disadvantaged schools may have less-capable teaching staffs. To the extent that this is true, adjusting scores for background characteristics may remove information about differences in school quality that policymakers hope to measure.

Some systems report both adjusted and unadjusted scores, or provide information so that users can compare a school with others that have similar student populations. California, for example, provides a decile ranking on its Academic Performance Index (API), which is a summary of test-score information that shows how a school is performing relative to all other schools in the state. In addition, each school is given a decile ranking based on similar schools, which indicates how well it is doing relative to other schools that serve comparable student populations and have similar resource constraints. Although the similar-schools ranking is not used as part of the state's accountability program, these rankings are often reported in local newspapers, and are sometimes cited by school personnel as evidence that a school is doing well even when it does not receive a high overall API.

Combining Results in Accountability Indices. In addition to determining how to report test scores to teachers, students, and parents, states with high-stakes accountability systems must devise strategies for summarizing scores and assigning a rating to the unit that is being held accountable, which is typically a school. These summary ratings are often called *accountability indices.* Although stakes for students have been increasing, most systems do not involve the construction of an accountability index for students. Instead, a student usually must meet one or more criteria, such as scoring above a particular cut score on one exit examination (as in Massachusetts) or on each of several examinations (as in New York). Therefore, we focus this discussion on school-level accountability indices.

Accountability indices range from fairly simple test-score averages to quite complicated sets of decision rules. Linn (2001), for example, discusses Florida's system of grading schools for accountability, which combines information about Florida Comprehensive Assessment Test (FCAT) scores in several subjects and dropout rates for high schools, and which takes into account both current performance and improvement. To receive a grade of A, a school must:

- Meet the following criteria in reading, writing, and math performance for the current year:
- At least 50 percent of students score Level 3 or above in reading on FCAT
- At least 50 percent of students score Level 3 or above in math on FCAT
- At least 67 percent of students score Level 3 or above in writing on FCAT.
- Test at least 95 percent of eligible students

- Maintain or improve the reading scores of its lowest-performing students (i.e., the percentage of students scoring in the lowest 25 percent in the state in reading must decrease or remain within 2 percentage points from the previous year)

- Demonstrate substantial improvement in reading and no substantial decline in math or writing scores (i.e., an increase of more than 2 percentage points in students scoring FCAT Level 3 and above; requirement is waived for some high-performing schools)

- Have a dropout rate no higher than one standard deviation above the previous year's state average or show improvement in the dropout rate from the previous year (high schools only) (Florida Department of Education, 2001).

As this example illustrates, the interpretation of a single grade or accountability "score" can be quite complex. Decisions about how to create an accountability index must weigh the importance of providing easily understood information against the need to incorporate multiple measures and levels of performance. Many of the reporting-related issues we discussed earlier are relevant to these decisions. Those responsible for developing and implementing accountability systems must decide whether the index used to determine a school's success or failure uses norm-referenced or criterion-referenced information, whether it takes into account the performance of subgroups of students, and whether information other than test scores (e.g., attendance or graduation rates) is included.

Regardless of the index chosen, policymakers must also choose an "evaluative standard"—that is, they must decide how performance on that index will be used to determine whether the performance of the unit (usually the school) is eligible for rewards or sanctions. We turn to this issue in the next section.

SETTING TARGETS FOR PERFORMANCE

A test-based accountability system requires that targets be set for performance of schools or other units that are subject to rewards or sanctions.[6] Current practice at the state and district level includes two broad approaches to setting targets, which we call "status" and "change" measures. *Status measures* compare a unit's performance at one point in time with a single standard, which may be a performance criterion set by a state, the average performance of similar units, or a historical average. *Change measures* compare a unit's performance at one time with some measure of prior performance.[7]

Measuring Status

Many state accountability systems (as well as federal legislation) have established moderate- or long-term targets that are applied to all schools, regardless of the level of achievement at which they start or of the conditions under which they operate. For example, numerous states have set a date by which all schools must have a specified percentage of students at or above one of the state's performance standards. The percentage and the standard used as a target vary; however, one recent study reported that "seven states specify that they expect 90 to 100 percent of students to reach proficiency, eight states specify they expect 60 to 85 percent to reach this level, and another eight states set the goal at 50 percent meeting the assessment target" (Goertz and Duffy, 2001, 20).

These rules create more-ambitious short-term targets for schools with initially lower performance. The rationale for this approach is the goal of holding all students and schools to the same high standards—a goal that is commonly expressed by politicians and educators alike. However, in the absence of clear explanations for initial differences in performance, it is not clear that greater expectations for lower-performing schools are necessarily realistic. Indeed, identical expectations for change are not necessarily realistic even for schools with identical initial performance. For example, consider two hypothetical schools that initially have identical levels of performance that are far below the long-term performance goal. One of

---

[6]We focus here on schools rather than individual students. Targets for students typically take the form of a cut score on a test. Procedures for setting cut scores were discussed earlier in this chapter.

[7]Decisions about whether to use status or change measures also arise in the construction of an accountability index, as the Florida example earlier illustrates.

these schools has a stable population of students, most of whom speak English as a native language, but has a weak curriculum and an unmotivated teaching force. The second school has an able and motivated teaching force but a student population that includes many recent immigrants who do not speak English as a native language and has a very high rate of transience, so teachers often have little time to work with a given student before he or she is tested. Faced with strong incentives to improve scores, these schools might show very different rates of gain.

In addition, the moderate- or long-term performance goals established by some states are typically arbitrary in the sense that they are not based on empirical information about performance, such as normative data about the performance of high-quality schools or research on the plausible effects of large-scale interventions. The resulting targets can be extremely high, particularly for initially low-scoring schools that are required to show more rapid gains than other schools. For example, Koretz and Barron (1998) analyzed the gains required by the Kentucky Instructional Results Information System (KIRIS) accountability system for much of the 1990s:

> The required thresholds would require gains in many cases of approximately two standard deviations or more over 20 years, and possibly three standard deviations in some extreme cases. Thus, in each two-year accountability cycle, schools would need to raise scores roughly 0.2 standard deviation or more. To obtain rewards would require somewhat more improvement, increasing the total required gain by roughly an additional 10 to 20 percent each biennium . . . These expected rates of change are by any standard very large—indeed, unprecedented in large-scale educational interventions (Koretz and Barron, 1998, 21).

Koretz and Barron argued that these unrealistically high targets may have contributed to the inflation of scores that they observed in Kentucky; they reasoned that teachers faced with targets they cannot reach by legitimate means will have strong incentives to cut corners in ways that may corrupt scores.

Measuring Change

This section describes three methods for measuring change in performance:

- The *cross-sectional* approach: comparing this year's fourth-graders with last year's fourth-graders

- The *quasi-longitudinal* approach: comparing this year's fourth-graders with last year's third-graders

- The *longitudinal* approach: linking individual student scores to compare students with themselves over time.

Linn (2001; see also Carlson, 2000) discusses several approaches to summarizing improvement in test scores to obtain change measures. The cross-sectional approach involves comparing students in a particular grade in the current year with those who were in that same grade in the previous year; e.g., comparing this year's fourth graders to last year's fourth graders.[8] This may be the only option for measuring change in states that test students only in nonconsecutive grades.

In the quasi-longitudinal approach, scores for students in a particular grade are compared with those for students in the prior grade that are obtained the previous year; e.g., this year's fourth-graders are compared with last year's third-graders. This approach represents an effort to track the same students over time, but without requiring student-level data.

The final approach, longitudinal, uses student-level data linked over time, producing a school-level index that synthesizes the actual test score gains achieved by students in that school. This is often called "value-added" evaluation because it attempts to measure the additional achievement, or value, added by a period of schooling by the unit in question.

---

[8] Note that the "cross-sectional" method is not cross-sectional in the usual sense of using data from only one point in time. Rather, it entails comparing cross-sectional summaries from two different cohorts in two different years. We use the terms "status" and "change" here to avoid confusion with Linn's use of the terms "cross-sectional" and "longitudinal."

Using longitudinally linked data may be particularly important in school systems with high mobility rates, in which case this year's fourth-graders and last year's third-graders may include many students who were not present both years and therefore were not consistently provided the quality of services offered by that school. However, in such cases the use of longitudinal data will result in the loss of data for some students and, if the highly mobile students also tend to be the lower performers, may not provide a full picture of student achievement at a particular school.

Although several states have testing programs that would permit the linking of individual student records over time, few have actually implemented such an approach. Nevertheless, interest in doing this linking is growing. The Tennessee Value Added Assessment System (TVAAS), which uses individual student data to evaluate the effectiveness of teachers (Sanders and Horn, 1998), has garnered widespread attention even though it is currently not used in the state's formal accountability system. One of the perceived strengths of these approaches is that they provide a method for tying student performance to individual teachers within a school, although the use of scores for evaluating teachers faces a number of technical and political hurdles.

REWARDS AND SANCTIONS

In this section, we briefly discuss the kinds of rewards and sanctions that are being adopted to hold schools, teachers, and students accountable for performance (for a recent state-by-state description, see Goertz and Duffy, 2001). In some states, although the number of those states is shrinking, consequences are presumed to result from simply publicizing scores. For example, parents and administrators can use scores to exert pressure on schools with low scores. Parents may also use information about test scores to decide where to buy houses or, in a choice-based system, where to send their children to school.

The increasing popularity of Web-based information has led many states to provide school-level information, or "report cards," to the public via the Internet. In addition to test scores, these report cards may include data on student enrollment, teacher qualifications, special programs, and other information that is likely to be of interest to the public. There is currently no substantial evidence on the effects of published report cards on parents' decisionmaking or on the schools themselves. Research in Florida suggests that the social stigma associated with that state's grading system (which uses letter grades of A through F) leads staff members at both low- and high-performing schools to target their instructional efforts toward maintaining a high grade, and that the stigmatizing effect of a low grade may be more important to teachers than are the threats of specific sanctions such as vouchers for private school tuition (Goldhaber and Hannaway, 2001).

A principal element in current education reform, however, is to tie specific rewards and sanctions to performance on tests rather than simply publish results. This trend is made evident by the recent changes in the testing programs of many states and some districts, and it is the focus of the NCLB Act.

School-Level Incentives

Many of the state policies put in place during the 1990s imposed test-based rewards and sanctions on schools or educators, but not on students. There are several general types of sanctions currently being used, and some are less severe than others. All states that sanction schools require low-performing schools to create and implement an improvement plan, or mandate that another entity, such as the state or a school district, do so. Harsher sanctions include placing a low-performing school on probation, removing a low-performing school's accreditation, withholding funding from a low-performing school, reconstituting a low-performing school, closing a low-performing school, taking over a low-performing school, and offering tuition vouchers to students at low-performing schools (Ziebarth, 2000).

It should be noted that some of these actions are not necessarily intended to be punitive and may in fact be helpful to schools. Targeting assistance, as well as resources, to low-performing schools may prove to be an effective strategy to remedy problems and promote improved achievement. Goldhaber and Hannaway (2001) found that in Florida, some low-performing schools that received resources as a result of poor performance used the money to reduce class sizes, provide new instructional materials and staff development, and offer after-school tutoring programs. This example illustrates how difficult it is to disentangle the effects of holding schools accountable from the effects of additional spending when trying to determine if test-based accountability improves achievement.

In addition to sanctions for low-performing schools, many states offer rewards to motivate and recognize schools whose students perform well. In 2001, 17 states rewarded schools for their performance on test scores. Most of the states offered some type of financial reward to the schools, and all of these states except five allowed the money to be used to reward teachers through bonuses. In addition, some states offer financial rewards to individual teachers based on the performance of students in their schools (Education Week, 2001). For example, in 2001, California awarded bonuses of up to $25,000 to teachers at schools whose students had demonstrated large test-score gains. These programs have not been in place long enough to permit a judgment of whether they are effective at motivating teachers and administrators.

Student-Level Incentives

More recently, a growing number of states and districts have turned to test-based consequences for students, either alone or in conjunction with consequences for schools or educators. Promotion and graduation may be tied to performance on state or district tests, and some states have proposed monetary rewards. As with the minimum competency testing movement of the 1970s, the most common form of serious consequences for students in current state testing systems is a requirement that students pass one or more tests to graduate from high school. As of 2000, more than half of the states had implemented or were developing some form of a high school exit exam, and several of these states planned to administer at least one such exam in each of the four core subjects of English, mathematics, science, and social studies. Other tested subjects include world languages, health, and the arts, although these subjects were much less common.

Many of these exit exams, like the tests administered at lower grades, are designed to provide a broad survey of achievement in a particular subject such as math or reading. Others, such as those planned in Virginia and Maryland, are end-of-course exams that assess achievement of the objectives of a particular course, such as algebra (see Olson [2001] for an overview of recent state initiatives). New York's new Regents examination system represents a new direction in curriculum-based high school testing. In the long-standing system that is now being replaced, students intending to attend college took the Regents examinations; the exam was not required for high school graduation. The tests were tied to specific yearlong courses, such as algebra, geometry, and trigonometry. The new Regents examinations, which are being phased in as a requirement for a high school diploma for all students in the state, are tied to curricular areas but not to specific courses. For example, the new lower-level mathematics test, Mathematics A, includes a considerable amount of basic algebra but is not restricted to algebra and is not tied to a specific course; it is expected that students will take the exam early in high school, but the courses preparing students for the exam may vary in content and length from one district or school to another.

Although there is widespread agreement among the public that students should be required to pass a test before receiving a diploma (Business Roundtable, 2001b), several states have recently delayed the implementation of their high school exit exams. Their main concern stems from low pass rates on initial administrations of the tests and the possible implications of denying diplomas to large numbers of students. In Arizona, for example, lawmakers recently voted to postpone the test-based graduation requirement until 2006, the fourth such postponement since 1996 (Bowman, 2001). The move was designed to give the state time to investigate the sources of poor student performance, explore possible alternative routes to diplomas for students who do not pass, and ensure that the curricula in place in the state's schools were providing the necessary skills to help students pass the test. The delay was controversial, with many critics arguing that it will derail the state's efforts to hold schools accountable for student performance. Faced with similar challenges, a number of other states have recently rescinded their decisions to impose exit examinations, delayed their implementation, or lowered their initial cut score for passing (Education Commission of the States, 2001).

Now, as in the 1970s, strict promotional-gates policies (i.e., the use of test scores to determine whether students are promoted to the next grade) are less common than high school exit exams at the state level.

Eighteen states have policies that incorporate students' scores on state or district assessments into decisions about retention in grade; two states have policies for retaining students solely on the basis of test scores. In addition, a number of large school districts, such as New York City and Chicago, have tied promotion to performance on a single test. Some states also mandate interventions for low-scoring students; these interventions may include summer school, tutoring, or other forms of supplemental instruction. And a few states provide performance incentives, such as scholarship money for high-scoring students. As with school-level accountability, the consequences of low test scores for students are not necessarily negative. The supplemental instruction that students receive may help ensure that those students do not fall through the cracks, especially if efforts are made to monitor the quality and effectiveness of the instruction.

Several professional organizations have cautioned against using a single test score to make high-stakes decisions about individuals (see, for example, American Educational Research Association [2000]). Many policymakers involved in the development of accountability systems have acknowledged the importance of including multiple measures of student and school performance, but there is disagreement on the meaning of "multiple measures." Several states use indicators other than test scores in their school-level accountability indices. These indicators typically include attendance and dropout rates. They are typically weighted much less heavily than test scores, however, and in some states, data limitations have prevented nontest indicators from being included at all. Also, while numerous states employ more than a single test in their assessment systems, a few include more than one test in their accountability system at a given grade. Thus, the experts' advocacy of multiple measures has not yet had a strong influence on the designs of state accountability systems.

One important distinction that should be made is the one between *compensatory models,* in which poor performance on one measure may be offset by good performance on another, and *conjunctive models,* in which meeting a target and receiving a reward (or avoiding a sanction) is contingent upon success on each of a set of measures. An example of a conjunctive model is one in which students must pass a reading test and a math test in addition to achieving a certain record of attendance in order to graduate; failure on one of these indicators would result in denial of a diploma. Although the system incorporates multiple measures, it is not consistent with professional guidelines because students may be prevented from graduating on the basis of a single score.

SUMMARY

In this chapter, we discussed ways in which the role of large-scale testing has evolved over the past several decades, and we presented descriptive information about current state tests and accountability systems. Current assessment policy has been shaped in large part by federal education legislation, and will likely continue to change markedly in response to the 2001 NCLB legislation.

Those responsible for developing test-based accountability systems face an array of often difficult decisions at all stages, including deciding what to test, choosing a form of testing, selecting methods for reporting results, creating an accountability index, and determining the rewards and sanctions that will be attached to performance. This chapter described variation in the decisions that states have made to address these issues. The major options at each stage all have their advantages and disadvantages. In some cases, we have noted that some choices bring with them serious disadvantages; we do this not to argue against any approach, but rather to help clarify the trade-offs inherent in these decisions. For example, developing a test specifically for a state can offer a means of ensuring alignment between the test and the state's standards but at the cost of not providing normative information that many parents, students, and educators find useful. Reporting test results only at the school level permits the use of matrix sampling, which offers better coverage of content and less incentive to narrow instruction, but at the cost of not providing reliable and valid scores for individual students.

Despite the well-publicized and specific requirements of the NCLB Act, state-level variation in assessment and accountability systems is likely to continue, and those who are responsible for designing those systems will face many of these trade-offs. Decisions should be informed by an understanding of the likely consequences of alternative approaches, and should take into consideration both the needs of various stakeholders and the constraints on resources. The details of how a system is implemented are critical for determining whether it will have beneficial or adverse consequences. In Chapter Six, we re-visit some of these issues and provide some suggestions for those who are involved in the design of test-based accountability systems.

Chapter Three

TECHNICAL CRITERIA FOR EVALUATING TESTS

Vi-Nhuan Le and Stephen P. Klein

- How do we know if a test supports content standards?

- How do we know if test scores reflect students' actual learning?

- How can we measure the fairness of the tests and the reliability of test scores?

The previous chapter discussed features of test-based accountability systems. The focus of this chapter is on the technical quality of the tests themselves. In this chapter, we discuss the three main technical criteria by which the technical quality of tests should be evaluated: reliability, validity, and fairness. We begin by defining reliability. We then discuss certain factors that affect reliability, ways to quantify reliability, and the two most common reliability indices. Next, we describe judgmental and quantitative evidence that can be used to assess a test's validity. This is followed by a discussion of fairness, which includes issues of bias as well as of comparability in opportunities for students to learn and demonstrate their knowledge. We conclude by discussing the trade-offs among reliability, validity, fairness, testing time, and costs. (The specifics of how to calculate relevant psychometric statistics can be found in standard texts on this topic; e.g., Crocker and Algina, 1986.)

FIRST, SOME BACKGROUND

As background for what follows, it is important to appreciate that a test contains only a sample of all the questions that could be asked in a subject matter area or "domain," such as fourth-grade mathematics. Test scores are only useful to the extent that they accurately reflect the students' mastery of the domain the test is designed to measure. In other words, is it reasonable to infer from the test results how well the students would have performed if they had been asked a much larger and broader sample of questions from the domain? In short, how well can we generalize from the test (which is a sample) to the domain itself? And, are the scores reasonably free from bias and the effects of chance? The answers to these questions depend on several factors, including the way in which the test is designed and constructed and the ways in which the scores are used.

Because tests are samples, the confidence that can be placed in their scores depends on how well the test covers the range of knowledge and skills it is supposed to measure. No test can measure everything in a domain. However, a well-designed test can provide useful (albeit not necessarily comprehensive) information about the domain it is supposed to assess. Consequently, two tests that are designed to measure the same domain can differ substantially in content coverage, format, and problem types. And, these differences can affect the quality of their scores and the interpretation of what they mean.

Test quality hinges not only on how well the test is designed and constructed, but also on how its scores are used. For example, if scores are used to make high-stakes decisions about individual students (such as whether they receive a high school diploma), then it is imperative that these scores be stable indicators of student performance. Such consistency is not as critical when the students' scores are used to assess the outcomes of an educational program because the effects of chance are more likely to be balanced out across students within a program.

SCORE RELIABILITY

Reliability refers to the degree to which a test's scores are free from various types of chance effects. One way to think about this is to answer the question: What is the likelihood that a student's score, proficiency level, or pass/fail status would change if that student took the same test again the next day or took another version (i.e., another "form") of it?

Reliability is a characteristic of the scores on a test as distinct from a characteristic of its questions. For example, a test that is much too difficult for a particular group to answer (and results in everyone picking answers at random) will produce very unreliable scores for this group even though it may yield highly reliable scores for the students for which the test was intended. In this section, we discuss the factors that affect score reliability, the main quantitative indices of reliability, and how the decision about what constitutes "adequate" reliability depends on how the scores are used.

Factors That Affect Score Reliability

A student's score, proficiency level, or pass/fail status on a test can vary from one form of that test to another (or from one day to the next on the same form) for reasons that have nothing to do with any learning or maturation that took place in between the test sessions. The four broad classes of factors that can lower score reliability are item sampling, transitory variables, rater agreement, and test length and format.

Item Sampling. Various questions can be constructed to assess student knowledge of a given topic. Some of these questions can be put into one form of a test while others can be put into another form. Although both of these sets of questions are designed to be comparable, a given student may do better on one set than on another set while the reverse may be true for another student. In short, a student's score may fluctuate as a function of the particular version of the test taken. By definition, such inconsistency lowers reliability.

For example, suppose an examinee studied the contributions made to women's rights by Susan B. Anthony but not those by Elizabeth Cady Stanton. Suppose further that one form of the test covers the women's suffrage movement by asking questions about Ms. Anthony while another form has questions about Ms. Stanton. The student who studied Ms. Anthony's contributions is likely to do better on the first form than on the second one while the reverse is true for someone who learned only about Ms. Stanton's contributions. Thus, a student's score may depend on the particular sample of questions that are asked about a topic and the nature of a student's knowledge about that subject. This "student by task interaction" lowers score reliability because it is a matter of chance which form of the test a student takes.

Transitory Factors. There are a host of factors that have the potential for affecting student scores on a particular administration of a test that are independent of the particular sample of questions that are asked. These factors—all of which have the potential for lowering score reliability—include whether the student was healthy or ill, relaxed or anxious, or rested or tired on the day the test was given; the time of day the test was given; the room lighting and other environmental conditions during the test; the degree of adherence to instructions and time limits; the quality of the test booklets and other materials; the encouragement that teachers and others gave to students to do well on the test; and other such factors. The extent to which such transitory variables actually affect scores (and thereby lower reliability) depends on other factors, such as the nature of any disturbances that occurred during the test session and each student's response to such disturbances.

Rater Agreement. Raters (also called readers or judges) are needed to score student responses to essay questions, performance tasks, and other types of open-ended test questions. The reliability of a student's score on a test is reduced if these raters disagree with each other in the score they assign to an answer (or if a rater assigns different scores to the same answer on different occasions).

There are three basic ways in which raters can differ from each other. They can have different average scores (i.e., some raters are more lenient than others), score spreads (i.e., how much they use the full range of possible scores), or relative standings (i.e., the extent to which they agree on which answers are better than others). Corresponding differences can also arise when a rater evaluates the same answers on different occasions. Many studies have shown that a high degree of rater agreement can be obtained if there is a well-constructed and field-tested scoring guide (or "rubric") and if the raters receive extensive training in the use of these guidelines (Shavelson, Baxter, and Gao, 1993).

High rater agreement by itself does not mean that the students' test scores are highly reliable. For instance, readers can agree perfectly with each other on the scores that should be assigned to the answers the students wrote to essay question number 1, but the scores on this question may not correlate with the scores these students earned on the test's other essay questions.

Test Length and Format. All other factors being equal, longer tests (e.g., those with more questions) yield more reliable scores than shorter ones. And, obtaining a highly reliable estimate of an individual student's proficiency level often requires asking a large number of questions. The reason longer tests usually produce more reliable scores than shorter ones is that longer tests can contain a larger sample of questions from the domain being assessed. This is analogous to the benefits derived from conducting an exit poll at 20 precincts rather than just 5 precincts.

Tests that rely on essay questions or other types of open-ended tasks generally require far more testing time per student to achieve a given level of score reliability than do multiple-choice tests (Dunbar, Koretz, and Hoover, 1991; Linn, 1993; Wainer and Thissen, 1993). This is especially so when computer adaptive tests are used (Hamilton, Klein, and Lorie, 2000). However, multiple-choice tests cannot assess certain types of knowledge and skills. That is one of the reasons why score reliability is not the sole criterion for evaluating test quality.

Quantifying Score Reliability

For users of test data, arguably the most important reliability concern is the degree of confidence that can be placed on the scores. In other words, a key issue is how dependable are the scores? While there are a number of different methods used to estimate reliability, the most widespread procedures are test-retest, alternate forms, internal consistency, and generalizability theory. These methods provide a reliability statistic that quantifies the inconsistency of scores, namely a reliability coefficient or standard error of measurement (SEM). The following discussion is intended to be a conceptual introduction to ways in which to estimate and quantify reliability. Readers interested in a more technical discussion are referred to Feldt and Brennan (1989).

Methods of Estimating Reliability. There are three generic ways of estimating reliability: alternate forms, test-retest, and internal consistency. The *alternate forms method* involves having each student take two forms of the test, and correlating their scores on these forms. The *test-retest method* involves the students taking the same form of the test on two different occasions and examining the correlation between their scores on these occasions. The *internal consistency method* looks at the correlation among all the different questions within a single form of the test (such as between the even and odd numbered questions) or among the items within each subtest or section.

Each approach has its own set of assumptions, advantages, and limitations. Consequently, the reliability coefficient obtained with one method may differ substantially from the coefficient obtained with another method. Some of the factors that could lead to different coefficients are how much the scores depend on how fast the student answers, the degree to which the items within a test measure the same skills and knowledge, and the amount of time between test administrations.

A drawback of the reliability procedures just described is that they do not differentiate among multiple sources of error. For example, suppose two raters judged student performance on two different tasks that were administered on two different testing occasions. Using test-retest, alternate forms, or internal consistency methods, test users would not know the extent to which score inconsistencies were due to differences in raters judging the tasks, differences in the difficulty of the tasks, or differences in transitory factors (e.g., student fatigue) across testing occasions. This problem can be addressed by conducting a *generalizability* study that explores multiple sources of error simultaneously.

A typical generalizability study might involve students answering the same or comparable questions on different occasions, with two or more readers grading each student's answers to two or more questions. Such a study provides separate estimates for the various error sources (i.e., raters, tasks, occasions, and other sources of error). One of the strengths of a generalizability study is that it can identify the most serious sources of error, and this information can be used to guide decisions about what steps need to be undertaken in order to ensure more dependable scores. For instance, large error components associated with raters suggest that more reliable scores can be obtained by increasing the number of raters, the training of raters, or both. However, generalizability studies often involve a lot more grading and testing than is typically present in most assessment programs.

Reliability Statistics. After reliability is estimated, this information is reported via a reliability statistic. One of the most common reliability statistics is the *reliability coefficient,* which is an index that takes on any value from 0.0 to 1.0. A reliability coefficient of 0.0 indicates that the scores are completely undependable (i.e., the scores are no better than chance scores), whereas a coefficient of 1.0 indicates that the scores are completely dependable. For instance, a test that has perfect alternate-forms reliability means that an examinee's relative standing on one form of the test is entirely consistent with that examinee's standing on another form of that test. In practice, reliability coefficients are never 1.0, although all tests should aspire to yield coefficients as close to 1.0 as possible.

The second major reliability statistic is the *standard error of measurement* (SEM). The SEM is a function of the reliability coefficient and the degree to which the scores on a test tend to spread out around the average score (i.e., the standard deviation of these scores).[1] The SEM is analogous to a margin of error in a public opinion poll. For example, if a student's score on a test is 75 and the test has a SEM of 4, then the chances are roughly two out of three that the student's "true" score will fall between 71 and 79 (although 75 remains the best estimate of that score). The SEM is often useful for judging whether small differences in scores on a test are meaningful. For example, in this case, a score of 75 is fairly comparable to a score of 77 but is not comparable to a score of 80.

In general, the reliability coefficient is most useful for comparing the score reliabilities on different tests, whereas the SEM is especially useful for comparing scores within a test or for assessing the margin of error around a passing score (because the SEM is only meaningful in terms of the score scale on that test). As noted later in this section, what constitutes "adequate" reliability depends on several factors,

---

[1]The size of the SEM for a given score depends on how close that score is to the test's mean score. The further the score is from the mean, the larger its SEM.

including whether the scores are used to make decisions about individual students versus educational programs.

Score Reliability and Decisionmaking

As noted at the beginning of our discussion on reliability, one way to think about reliability is in terms of the likelihood that the test would result in the same pass/fail decision about a student (or put that student in the same proficiency category) regardless of the particular form of that test the student took (or whether the student took the same test at one time or another). A high degree of consistency in making that decision would coincide with the commonsense usage of the term reliability. However, the story is bit more complicated because the chance of making the same decision is also a function of the passing rate. Specifically, it is difficult to be inconsistent if almost everyone passes or almost everyone fails. On the other hand, score reliability is a particularly important consideration when the passing rate is anywhere between 25 and 75 percent.

Table 3.1 illustrates this relationship. It shows the percentage of students whose pass/fail status would change (i.e., from pass to fail or fail to pass) if they just took another form of the same test (or took the same test again). The table shows that the percentage of students whose pass/fail status would change is a function of both the passing

Table 3.1

Percentage of Students Whose Pass/Fail Status Would Change as a Function of the Passing Rate and Score Reliability

Percent Passing	Score Reliability									
	0.00	0.10	0.20	0.30	0.40	0.50	0.60	0.70	0.80	0.90
90	19	18	17	16	15	13	12	11	9	6
80	32	30	28	27	25	23	20	17	14	10
70	42	39	37	35	31	29	25	22	17	12
60	48	45	42	39	36	32	29	25	20	14
50	50	47	44	40	37	33	30	26	21	14
40	48	45	42	39	36	32	29	25	20	14
30	42	40	38	35	32	29	26	22	18	13
20	32	30	28	27	25	23	20	18	14	10
10	19	18	17	16	15	13	12	11	9	6

SOURCE: Klein and Orlando (2000).

rate and score reliability. For example, suppose a large urban school district decides that it will promote third-grade students to the fourth grade only if they are able to earn a certain score on a reading test. Those who fail must go to summer school to take remedial instruction in reading. Suppose further that 70 percent of the district's 5,000 third graders meet this standard and that the test used to determine whether the standard is met has an alternate-forms reliability coefficient of 0.70 in this population of students.

Under the conditions just described, about 22 percent of the children would have their pass/fail status affected if they simply took another form of the same test. In other words, about 11 percent of the 5,000 third graders who were initially identified as having to participate in the summer school program would now be exempt from having to attend, whereas another 11 percent (or 550 children) would be in the opposite situation. Put another way, over a third of the 1,500 students who were required to take the summer program would not have been so classified if they had simply taken another form of the test. Increasing score reliability to 0.90 would cut the number of inconsistent classifications almost in half.

Examples like the one above illustrate the importance of score reliability when test scores are used to make important decisions about individual students. In contrast, score reliability is usually less a concern when scores are aggregated to the classroom or educational program level. This is because aggregating over large groups of examinees means that many (but not necessarily all) of the item sampling and transitory factors are balanced across students.

Whether test scores are considered "adequately" reliable depends on several factors, chief among them are the particular policies that are adopted for using those scores. Scores that are used to make decisions about individual students will require higher levels of reliability than scores that are used to make decisions about educational programs. For example, Koretz et al. (1994) found that the scoring of student portfolios in Vermont was too inconsistent to yield accurate interpretations about individual students, but that the results at the state level were reliable enough to monitor changes over time. Test users who wish to make decisions about individual students should be aware that a student's score is likely to vary much more across test administrations (i.e., have a much larger SEM) than will the mean of that student's classroom or school.

VALIDITY

Validity refers to the extent to which the scores on a test provide accurate information for the decisions that will be based on those scores (Cronbach, 1971; Messick, 1989). Validity is not an inherent characteristic of a test. It is a characteristic of the decisions that are based on the test scores and the subsequent uses of those scores (Cronbach, 1988). A given test may provide accurate information for one purpose but not for another. For instance, a test that requires examinees to multiply single-digit numbers can provide valid information about the multiplication skills of second graders, but it is not a valid measure of their proficiency in arithmetic because it does not assess addition, subtraction, or division skills. Moreover, if this same test is given to adults, it is probably more a measure of their perceptual speed than their multiplication skills.

The term validity is often used to encompass the reasonableness of both score-based inferences and the effects of a given use of a test, which are then referred to as "consequential validity." For clarity, we consider only the quality of inferences here. We consider the effects of testing separately in Chapter Four.

The kinds of interpretations that can be supported by test scores depend on the knowledge and skills that the test is supposed to assess. Thus, validity is necessarily related to test development. Test development consists of three main stages: *framework definition, test specification,* and *item selection* (National Research Council, 1998). In the framework definition stage, test developers use content standards to describe the scope of the domain to be assessed. The next stage involves the development of test specifications that delineate how the domain will be represented. In addition to circumscribing the format, time limit, and number of items that appear from each of the standards to be measured, test specifications may also describe the level and type of cognitive processes that students will need to draw upon in answering questions correctly. In the final stage, items are developed and selected to meet the test specifications. As will be discussed in the following sections, each of these stages affects the validity of the test.

The remainder of this section discusses the different types of judgmental and quantitative evidence that can be used to support the validity of a test's scores and the validity of scores and gains under high-stakes conditions.

Forms of Validity Evidence

In the past, it was common to think of the evaluation of tests as comprising several different "types" of validity tied to specific forms of evidence. For example, information on the appropriateness of test content was labeled "content validity" and information on the accuracy with which scores predict future performance was called "predictive validity." This terminology, however, has been largely abandoned because it is now generally recognized that the validity of an inference is a unified concept. Different types of evidence can contribute to that unitary judgment, and they should be taken together to evaluate the soundness of the interpretations with respect to the purposes of the test. There are still some instances in which people refer to specific types of validity; for example, the notion of "instructional validity," i.e., the degree to which students have had the opportunity to learn the content of an achievement test, still has wide currency.[2] However, these exceptions do not contradict the general notion that validity represents an integrative summary of evidence.

We next discuss different kinds of validity evidence, which are broadly categorized as those based on expert judgment and on quantitative data. This discussion is intended to be illustrative rather than comprehensive.

Evidence Based on Expert Judgment. A first step in evaluating the support a score provides for a given inference is to evaluate the content of the test. The framework and specifications for a test reflect the

---

[2]Some measurement experts argue that "instructional validity," while important, should not be considered an aspect of validity at all; whether a test adequately supports an inference about students' proficiency in a given area does not depend on whether the students were taught that material in school. In practice, whether instructional validity is relevant is in large part a function of the kinds of inferences that are being made on the basis of scores (e.g., whether scores are interpreted as indicators of student academic attainment or of school effectiveness).

inferences the test designers intend the test to support. Thus, if the test is being used for purposes consistent with that intent, evaluation of the consistency of the test's content with its framework and specifications can provide useful validity evidence.

For state testing programs, the test specifications are designed to capture the state's content standards. Most state testing programs convene a group of content experts to ensure that the test specifications reflect the content standards, and that the test items reflect the test specifications. The steps are particularly important if commercially developed exams are used to monitor student progress toward state standards because such exams are not designed to reflect the content standards of any particular state. Some states, such as Delaware, use only test items that have been judged to address a content standard in their calculations of a standards-based score. Other states, such as California, augment the commercially developed exams with additional items that were developed to improve the overall alignment of the combined test with the content standards.

Because tests are samples from a content domain, they may omit or poorly represent some important aspects of the larger domain. This failure to capture the entire domain is called *construct underrepresentation*. If a test fails to capture important elements of the domain, scores can only justify narrow or qualified conclusions about performance. For instance, a test that is intended to assess knowledge of 19th-century American history but omits items about the Civil War provides an incomplete picture of students' knowledge of that period of history. Content experts can help safeguard against construct underrepresentation by identifying whether any of the excluded or de-emphasized material represents important elements whose absence would seriously compromise the proposed interpretations.

Similarly, experts may find that the final set of test items includes content that is not pertinent to the intended inferences. This is called *construct-irrelevant content*. Some states, such as Maryland, assess student knowledge of mathematics with items that require written explanations. This may be a source of construct-irrelevant content because a low score in mathematics may indicate a lack of verbal skills to communicate an answer as opposed to a lack of mathematics knowledge (Hambleton et al., 2000). If that occurred it would undermine validity because a student who is actually comparable to a peer in terms of mastery of mathematics may receive a lower score solely because of differences in writing ability.[3] There also are issues regarding how much weight is given to different topics within a test (and because of statistical reasons, this weight may not coincide exactly with the number of items allocated to each topic).

Although content-related evidence is both essential and intuitively appealing, it has numerous limitations:

- First, test specifications are sometimes intentionally vague so as to avoid fostering overly narrow assessment goals (Popham, 1992).

- Second, the apparent content of an item, even when judged by an expert, is not always a trustworthy guide to the skills and knowledge that students will actually bring to bear in answering it. Research suggests it is difficult to determine the skills that are needed to answer a given item correctly by simply inspecting the surface features of the question (Hamilton, Nussbaum, and Snow, 1997). Instead, other methods such as interview procedures that ask students to "think aloud" as they solve the test items may be needed to provide evidence that the cognitive processes assumed to be underlying a given item are in fact elicited.

- Third, validity evidence about how well the test content corresponds with the test specifications may not be the most appropriate evidence in all situations. For example, when inferences attached to test scores are not those intended by the test's developers, the match between the test's framework and the test content is not as important as whether the test content can justify the *actual* (as opposed to intended) inferences.

  For example, the SAT I is designed to predict subsequent performance in college. Although some high school curriculum is included in the content, the SAT I is not intended to measure mas-

---

[3]Whether assessing mathematics achievement with written explanations constitutes construct irrelevance depends upon how mathematics achievement is defined. If mathematics achievement is defined to include the ability to communicate mathematics concepts in writing, then writing would probably *not* be considered construct-irrelevant content.

tery of high-school curricula. Despite caveats from the sponsor of the SAT I that "it is completely inappropriate to use the [SAT I] as a measure of comparison between states, school systems, or schools" (Toch, 1984), the U.S. Department of Education nevertheless published the famous "wall charts," which used state average SAT I scores as a measure of the quality of states' educational systems (Ginsburg, Noell, and Plisko, 1988).[4] Because the content of the SAT I is not intended to represent what students are taught in school, scores cannot adequately support inferences about how well that material has been taught or learned (and there are large differences across states in the characteristics of the students who choose to take this test). Although the wall charts are gone, misuse of the SAT I and other admissions test scores continues to occur in various contexts. Thus, a key aspect of validation is clarifying whether the actual inferences drawn from test scores can be supported by the test content and its empirical relationships with other variables, as well as whether those inferences are consistent with the purposes for which the test was designed.

The above example underscores the importance of validating each proposed use of a test. Although it may be tempting to use an existing test for multiple purposes, a test developed and validated for one purpose cannot be assumed to be valid for another because the test content may not lend itself to interpretations other than the ones for which it was originally intended. Therefore, extreme caution should be exercised when test scores are used for purposes for which they have yet to be validated.[5]

Evidence Based on Quantitative Data. Because content evidence alone may not provide a sufficient gauge of the support a test score provides for a given inference, it is often important to examine empirical evidence based on actual performance on the test.[6] Two of the

---

[4]During this time, the SAT I was known as the SAT.

[5]In some instances, it may be necessary to conduct reliability and validity studies after the test has been administered, but before the scores are used to make decisions about individuals or programs.

[6]Although there are published standards to guide validity investigations, there are no clear-cut rules regarding what evidence is important in what contexts. For example, in a court case related to the California Basic Educational Skills Test for teachers, the

most important types of empirical evidence are (1) the pattern of relationships among the scores on different measures (including the one being investigated) and (2) the pattern of relationships among the items within a test.

Pattern of Relationships Among Measures. The kinds of skills and knowledge a test is thought to assess provide a guide to the patterns of relationships among measures that should be found. A test that purports to assess certain kinds of skills should show stronger relationships with other measures that assess those same skills than with measures that assess different skills (Campbell and Fiske, 1959). Scores from a mathematics test, for instance, should show stronger relationships with scores from another mathematics test than with scores from a reading test. This type of evidence, called *convergent-discriminant evidence,* has played an important role in recent years in evaluating large-scale assessments. Yen and Ferrara (1997) conducted a convergent-discriminant analysis of Maryland's state test, the Maryland School Performance Assessment Program (MSPAP), and found that MSPAP reading scores showed as strong a relationship to the math scores from the Comprehensive Test of Basic Skills/4 (CTBS/4) test as they had with the CTBS/4 reading scores. This result, which may have stemmed in part from the interdisciplinary nature of the MSPAP, raises possible concerns about the MSPAP's validity (Hambleton et al., 2000). Specifically, the math scores appear to be heavily influenced by a student's reading skills.

Depending on the inferences they are used to support, scores on tests can be compared with a variety of variables (i.e., not just the score on other tests). For example, the SAT I and the ACT composite are used to predict performance in college. Therefore, the most common approach to assessing the validity of inferences supported by these tests is to assess how well they correlate with grades in college. This is most often done by examining the prediction of freshman-year grade point average (GPA), but studies have also looked at cumulative GPA over a longer period (Baron and Norman, 1992), persistence in college (Wilson, 1980), and graduation rates (Astin,

---

federal court held that content validation alone was sufficient for establishing the validity of a certification or employment test; i.e., criterion-related evidence was not required to determine whether the test scores were valid for the purposes for which they were being used (Mehrens, 1999).

Tsui, and Avalos, 1996). It is also important to evaluate whether the criterion measure that the test is designed to predict (such as first-year grades in college) is itself a reliable indicator of student performance and whether the test provides equally accurate predictions across groups (because differential prediction may suggest test bias). This is discussed in more detail later in this chapter in the section on fairness.

Relationships Within Measures. Many testing programs report scores separately by skill or by knowledge type, often called "subtest" or "subscale" scores. It is not uncommon, for example, to find mathematics performance reported as two scores, such as "problem solving" and "computation." An implicit assumption in reporting subscale scores is that there are sets of items within the test that measure the distinct skills included in each subscale. In order to explore whether this assumption is warranted, an examination of the interrelationships among individual test items needs to be undertaken. If a test does indeed justify separate subscale scores, then items that measure the same skill will behave more like each other than like items on another scale. If all items show similar relationships to each other, then the test does not support interpretations based on subscale scores, and a total score should be reported instead.[7]

Validity of Scores and Gains Under High-Stakes Conditions

One area aspect of validity that has drawn increasing attention in recent years is the validity of inferences attached to high-stakes measures. A particularly serious threat to the validity of such inferences is the risk that the scores will become inflated. That is, increases in test scores are considerably larger than increases in student proficiency, so that inferences about student learning are biased. Score inflation can occur, for example, if teachers focus unduly on the specific content of a test at the cost of de-emphasizing untested material that is nevertheless important to the curriculum. Score inflation can also arise when teachers coach students by focusing on incidental aspects

---

[7]There are exceptions to this principle. For example, while the pattern of correlations among items may coincide with the intended subscales when the student is the unit of analysis, it still may be possible that the subscales may vary as a function of schools or educational programs.

of a test, such as the particular rubrics used in scoring. Various forms of cheating also cause score inflation.

Score inflation is a particular concern when assessments are used to support inferences about *gains* in student performance. Under high-stakes conditions, scores may become progressively more inflated over time. Inflation of gains, however, can arise even in the absence of score inflation. For example, if an assessment is sufficiently novel, initial scores may be misleadingly low because students may not understand the directions or the kinds of responses that are expected of them. In this case, students' increasing familiarity with the test may mean that after one or two years scores are more accurate. Nonetheless, the *change* in scores from the starting point to the more accurate ending point would be exaggerated. In many instances, however, inflated gains arise from score inflation at the end of the period being considered, as opposed to unduly low scores when the assessment was first administered.

To evaluate possible score inflation, it is necessary to have some basis for comparing the level of scores. This can be done in at least two ways. In one district, Koretz et al. (1991) used national norms to place the results of two tests on the same scale and then compared mean scores across tests at one time. They also looked at trends over time within a single test. Both methods showed sizable score inflation. The more common approach, however, has been to compare trends on two tests. The logic of this approach is that gains on a high-stakes test should generalize to other measures. Although one would not expect perfect agreement (because even tests designed to measure similar domains differ), gains on a high-stakes test, if they are a valid indicator of improved student performance, ought to be reflected to a substantial degree in score gains on other measures that assess similar skills. For example, Koretz and Barron (1998) found that gains in mathematics scores in Kentucky during the 1990s on the high-stakes Kentucky Instructional Results Information System (KIRIS) assessment were nearly four times larger than the gains in Kentucky on the National Assessment of Educational Progress (NAEP). Similarly, Hambleton et al. (1995) found that Kentucky's initial rapid gains on the KIRIS reading assessment were not reflected in that state's NAEP reading scores. Klein et al. (2000) found similar results for the statewide achievement tests that are used in Texas.

Research on the inflation of gains remains too limited to indicate how prevalent the problem is. However, most studies that have specifically examined relevant evidence have found score inflation, and it has usually been severe. Thus, the research to date suggests that inferences based on scores from high-stakes tests should be validated using methods that are sensitive to score inflation.

FAIRNESS

Appropriate interpretations of test scores require that the test be fair to all takers. That is, the test should produce the same score for two test-takers who are of the same proficiency level. Unrelated characteristics of the test-takers, such as gender, ethnicity, or physical disabilities, and differences in administrative conditions should not affect the scores test-takers receive. Like validity, fairness is not an inherent property of the test but depends upon the use of the test. For a testing system to be fair, there are three key requirements: (1) the items and the test must be free of bias; (2) examinees must have comparable opportunities to demonstrate their knowledge and skills (i.e., there must be equitable treatment during the process of testing); and (3) examinees must have sufficient opportunity to learn the tested material (i.e., unless the purposes of the testing program include identifying students who have not had that opportunity). We next discuss each of these requirements.

Bias-Free Items and Tests

It is not uncommon for educators, policymakers, and the public to assume that a test is biased if there are large differences in average scores among groups. However, group differences in test scores may simply indicate that the groups differ in the knowledge, skills, and abilities that are being tested. Thus, freedom from bias does not necessarily entail score equality. By way of analogy, a fair test of some aspects of physical strength would not show that women and men are on average equally strong, but to be fair, it must give the same rating to individuals with comparable strength regardless of their gender.

Item Bias. Developers of most large-scale tests take a number of steps to detect and prevent bias on individual items. They have panels review the test to confirm that the items do not contain offensive or otherwise inappropriate language for various groups. They ensure that the exam corresponds to its test specifications and its curriculum frameworks or guidelines. They also may conduct statistical studies (i.e., *differential item functioning* [DIF] *analysis*) to flag questions that do not function in the same manner across groups. Specifically, DIF analysis flags an item when students who have the same total score on the test but belong to different groups have different probabilities of answering the item correctly. Although the presence of DIF in and of itself does not necessarily indicate that the item is flawed, some of the items flagged by the DIF analysis may be reviewed and excluded from the test before final scores are computed.

DIF analyses may be especially useful for suggesting sources of group differences on particular types of items. To illustrate, one of the items on a basic skills test for teachers in California asked, "How many half-pint servings are there in 5 gallons of milk?" White and black candidates performed better on this item than would be expected given their scores on the remaining items of the exam and the overall difficulty of this item among all candidates. The opposite was true for Hispanic and Asian candidates. It was hypothesized that Hispanic and Asian candidates were less familiar with the English system of measurement, and an item about the metric system would have shown the reverse pattern of group differences.

Whether information about group differences should be used in the test development process is open to debate. It is certainly true that the use of certain formats and content can affect the magnitude of group differences (Stocking et al., 1998; Willingham and Cole, 1997). For example, the extent to which gender differences in mathematics are manifested depends in part on the test's emphasis on reasoning skills (Harris and Carlton, 1993). Although some researchers believe it is the responsibility of test developers to select content that minimizes group differences while maintaining validity (Cole and Zieky, 2001), there has yet to be a consensus among the measurement community on whether group differences should be an explicit criterion when choosing test content.

Differential Prediction. A common method for examining bias in a test involves examining the predictive power of the test for different groups. This method is especially important when tests are used for the purpose of predicting who will do well in a future endeavor. For example, an increasing number of states are developing or are already using exams to certify that students have met the standards for high school graduation (Heubert and Hauser, 1999). There also is interest in using the scores on such tests for determining a student's eligibility for admission to state colleges and universities; i.e., as a replacement for the SAT I and ACT exams.

If high school graduation exams are to be used for these purposes, and if the large differences in scores (and passing rates) among racial/ethnic groups persist on these tests, then test developers will need to show that these differences do not stem from the exams being "biased" against the minority groups. One of the standard ways of examining this issue is to investigate whether minority and nonminority students with the same admission test scores do equally well in college. In general, if minority students do better, then the test is considered to be biased against them, whereas if they do less well than their nonminority classmates, then the test is biased in favor of the minority students. Previous research suggests that the latter outcome is much more likely to occur than the former (Linn, 1982).

Comparable Opportunities to Demonstrate Knowledge

Fairness requires that all examinees be afforded appropriate and equitable testing conditions. Standardization of administration conditions, which is common in most large-scale testing systems, is designed to ensure fair treatment by allowing all examinees to have the same amount of time to take the test, to receive the same instructions, and to take the test in comparable physical environments. In some instances, students are provided accommodations because they have disabilities or other challenges that prevent them from fully demonstrating their knowledge and skills under normal testing conditions. The accommodations are intended to offset the influence of construct-irrelevant factors on performance but, as we discuss next, have raised some validity questions in some instances.

Disabilities and Accommodations. The use of accommodations in large-scale testing has increased partly due to growing pressures to include all students in the assessment program and changes in the law stemming from the Americans with Disabilities Act. As is often mandated by a student's Individualized Education Plan (IEP), disabled students are granted accommodations to remove temporary or permanent disability-related barriers to performance that are ancillary to the construct the assessment is designed to measure. Test-based accountability policies have also contributed to increased attention to testing accommodations, as many states have sought to include students who had traditionally been exempted from testing requirements.

Currently, many state testing programs are struggling with ways in which disabled students can be accommodated. The major challenge is to balance students' needs for accommodations while maintaining comparability of score interpretations for students who have taken the test under standard conditions. A few states allow students to take state achievement tests under conditions that do not maintain score comparability (Consortium for Policy Research in Education, 2000). In Delaware, for example, some students are allowed to have the passages or text read to them during the reading test. Other states, such as Massachusetts and Maryland, have developed alternative assessments, such as portfolios, to be submitted in lieu of the state achievement test.

Relatively little is known about how testing accommodations affect score validity, and the few studies that have been conducted on the subject have had mixed results. Tippets and Michaels (1997) studied item interrelationships for accommodated and nonaccommodated students on the MSPAP and found the relationships to be comparable across the two groups. Similarly, Rock, Bennet, and Kaplan (1987) found that accommodated SAT I administrations were comparable to nonaccommodated administrations with respect to item interrelationships and reliability.

Other studies have found that accommodations may have been applied in ways that diminished validity. In one such case, disabled subgroups who had received accommodations demonstrated implausibly high scores, outperforming nondisabled students by nearly one-half a standard deviation (Koretz, 1997). The effect disappeared when the test was administered two years later, but it is impossible to determine what caused the change (Koretz and Hamilton, 2000). More research is needed to understand the sources of these findings.

Limited English Proficient Students and Accommodations. Because every test necessarily entails language to some degree, the performance of limited English proficient (LEP) students reflects factors that are ancillary to the intended construct and may result in underestimating their knowledge.[8] To circumvent this problem, many state testing programs offer accommodations that range from extending time limits to allowing the test instructions to be read orally in the student's dominant language (Consortium for Policy Research in Education, 2000).

A few states, including Vermont, New York, and New Mexico, offer versions of their assessments in languages other than English. Administering non-English versions of a measure has proved problematic, particularly because of equivalence problems. A translated test may not be comparable in content or rigor (and hence validity) as the original version because many words do not have the same frequency rates or difficulty levels across languages. Studying the comparability of an NAEP test that had been translated to Spanish, Anderson, Jenkins, and Miller (1996) concluded that comparisons across different language versions of a test were not possible because of substantial translation problems, including confusing language, varying vocabulary meanings, and increased potential for misunderstanding by LEP students. Other studies have reported that translated versions may be longer than the English version, thereby placing more demands on memory (Valencia and Rankin, 1985).

Beyond lack of translation equivalency, it cannot be assumed that a score obtained from the translated version should be interpreted in the same way as if it were obtained from the original test because test items may not function in the same manner. Studies have shown that psychometric properties are not always robust across the two languages, and in some cases, the translated items show poorer technical quality (Anderson, Jenkins, and Miller, 1996). As with the research on students with disabilities, more work is needed to understand how to interpret scores from these tests and how to develop tests that provide valid measures of achievement for all students.

---

[8]Language and reading tests are exceptions to this concern.

Opportunities to Learn. For tests that are used to deny or award students a high school diploma or that have other high-stakes outcomes for students, equity concerns require that all examinees have had sufficient exposure to the material on the test. The landmark Debra P. v. Turlington (1981) decision established that legally defensible high school graduation tests must have "instructional or curricular validity."[9] That is, students should have had an opportunity to learn the skills and gain the knowledge that the test is designed to measure.

It is unclear how to evaluate whether students have had an opportunity to learn the tested material. Some believe instructional validity should hinge on the actual instruction students receive rather than the formal written curriculum (Airasian and Madaus, 1983). In other words, it is not enough for the test content to reflect the content standards; instead, there must be evidence that the content was actually delivered within the classrooms. However, given that it may be impossible to show that every student was exposed to the necessary content, it has been argued that aligning tests to the published content standards is sufficient for demonstrating opportunity to learn. These issues are far from resolved, and the increasing emphasis on student-level accountability may lead to additional litigation.

Opportunity-to-learn issues are relevant not only to individual students but also to schools and school systems. Differences in test scores across schools with students who seem to be similarly situated may signal differences in educational opportunity. For that and other similar reasons, a state may want to administer tests to all students in order to help identify educational programs that are not providing sufficient educational opportunities. The fact that some students have not received opportunities to learn the content covered on a test should not prevent the testing of that content, although this lack of opportunity does influence the interpretation and use of the test scores. In this situation, scores may provide useful information about the effectiveness of different school programs, but in the interest of fairness, the scores should not be used to make high-stakes decisions about individual student mastery.

---

[9]See Phillips (1993) for a discussion of the Debra P. v. Turlington court decision.

TRADE-OFFS: TESTING TIME, COSTS, AND OTHER FACTORS

How test scores are used affects decisions about test design, which in turn affect decisions about content coverage, test length, format (multiple-choice versus essay and other open-response formats), administration and scoring procedures, and other factors. And, all of these decisions are likely to affect reliability, validity, fairness, testing time, costs, and other variables. For example, if scores are used to make high-stakes decisions about individual students, such as whether they are promoted, then a high degree of score reliability is needed. However, obtaining the score reliability that is needed to make decisions about individuals usually requires a substantial amount of testing time per student (which drives up costs) and/or narrowing the range of content standards that are assessed (such as not assessing those standards that require open-ended responses).

In contrast, if the scores are used to assess program effectiveness, then adequate score reliability can often be obtained with far less testing time per student and with greater validity. This result is achieved by having some students answer one set of questions and having other students answer other sets. As was discussed in Chapter Two, this strategy, which is called "matrix sampling," may increase validity because it facilitates obtaining a more comprehensive assessment of the students' knowledge and skills with less testing time than would be feasible had every student responded to every question. That is why a number of large-scale testing programs, such as NAEP, use matrix sampling. It is also why these programs do not report scores for individual students; i.e., such scores are not reliable enough for making decisions about individuals because a given student may see questions from only a small proportion of the content domain that the total test is assessing.

When test scores are used for making decisions about both individuals and programs, and when the testing time and other resources that are available for assessment activities are limited (as they almost always are), then there has to be some compromise among score reliability, validity, and costs. For example, a district may purchase a commercially developed test that is not especially well aligned with its standards, but which provides reliable scores in a relatively short amount of testing time and at a price the district can afford.

Tasks such as essays or performance assessments may be seen as more "authentic" indicators of student performance than multiple-choice tests and they can assess certain skills that are not measured well with the multiple-choice format. However, compared with multiple-choice items, the answers to open-response questions are much more costly to score (Stecher and Klein, 1997) and those scores are generally less reliable per hour of testing time (Wainer and Thissen, 1993).

Trade-offs in test design may also affect fairness. Girls, for example, tend to earn higher scores than boys on essay tests while the reverse is true on multiple-choice tests (Bolger and Kellaghan, 1990; Breland et al., 1994; Mazzeo, Schmitt, and Bleistein, 1993). Decisions about test design can therefore influence differences in scores among groups (Klein et al., 1997).

Issues regarding trade-offs with fairness also arise in decisions about releasing test questions to the public. For instance, many policymakers would like to have parents and teachers review a test before it is used so that they can provide input on what is assessed. Others would like a test's questions disclosed at least after the exam is administered so that they can check the accuracy of scoring keys and rubrics as well as to have guidance for better aligning curriculum and instruction with what is assessed. Indeed, that was how a significant error was discovered in the scoring key on a state's high school graduation test. However, releasing questions can lead to abuses that seriously undermine test validity (Cizek, 1998). For example, if in the weeks leading up to a state exam, students are taught how to solve the particular types of math problems that appear on this test, then their scores on the exam will reflect this specialized knowledge, but contrary to the purpose of the test, these scores will not generalize to the larger content domain that the test is designed to measure. In short, the scores will not be valid indicators of the students' mastery of the domain.

One partial solution to the disclosure dilemma that strives to maintain both validity and fairness involves (1) releasing a sample of the test's questions, (2) adding further safeguards to protect against scoring key problems, and (3) calibrating the next version of the test to the previous one through a set of secure items that are used on both tests. Another approach is to use a computer-based testing system in which students in the same classroom answer different questions that are drawn from the same bank of thousands of questions that are released but constantly updated and expanded (Hamilton, Klein, and Lorie, 2000).

CONCLUSION

With the increasing reliance on test scores as instruments of educational policy reform, it becomes more important than ever that tests are technically sound. To conclude this chapter, we summarize some of the key points in evaluating and using tests.

Tests should be evaluated relative to the purpose for which the scores are used. A test that is valid for one purpose may not be valid for another purpose. For example, tests that are used to evaluate the effectiveness of a given educational program may not be appropriate for making high-stakes decisions about individual student mastery. Similarly, test scores that are considered reliable enough to hold schools accountable may not be sufficiently reliable to make decisions about individual students.

Test scores are not a definitive measure of student knowledge or skills. An examinee's score can be expected to vary across different versions of a test because of differences in the particular sample of items that are asked, differences in the way graders evaluate student responses, and differences in transitory factors, such as the examinee's attentiveness on the day the test was taken. For these reasons, no single test score can be a perfectly dependable indicator of student performance, and high-stakes decisions about individuals should be based on factors other than the score on a single test (American Educational Research Association, American Psychological Association, and National Council on Measurement in Education, 1999).

It is important to recognize that decisions about test design (i.e., decisions on test length, item format, content coverage, and other considerations) require trade-offs with respect to reliability, validity, fairness, and costs. For instance, tests that include essay items may assess certain skills that cannot be measured with multiple-choice items, but are also more costly and less reliable per hour of testing, and in some cases may give female test-takers a relative advantage over male test-takers. Longer tests are generally more reliable and can sample a wider range of content than shorter tests. They also can provide more diagnostic information about student strengths and weaknesses. However, longer tests require more student testing time, which is time that is typically taken away from instruction. Thus, decisions about test design should be informed by the ways in which scores will be used and by resource constraints as well.

The issues discussed in this chapter regarding reliability, validity, and fairness highlight some of the many challenges that are faced by those who develop measures, implement test-based accountability systems, and use test results to make decisions about students and educational programs. Because test scores are numeric, they are often assumed to have a degree of precision that is not always justified. That is why those who use test scores to make decisions need to evaluate the technical characteristics of those scores relative to the purpose or purposes for which the scores are used. This evaluation is needed to make informed decisions about what the scores actually mean and how much confidence can be placed in them.

Chapter Four

CONSEQUENCES OF LARGE-SCALE, HIGH-STAKES TESTING ON SCHOOL AND CLASSROOM PRACTICE

Brian M. Stecher

- Why should we care about the effects of testing?

- What research has been done about the effects of high-stakes testing?

- What are the positive and negative effects of testing on classrooms? On schools?

This chapter examines the consequences of high-stakes testing on the educational system. We focus on the effects of high-stakes tests on students, teachers, and principals because the evidence of these effects is comparatively strong. High-stakes testing may also affect parents (e.g., their attitudes toward education, their engagement with schools, and their direct participation in their child's learning) as well as policymakers (their beliefs about system performance, their judgments about program effectiveness, and their allocation of resources). However, these issues remain largely unexamined in the literature. As a result, this chapter concentrates on the impact of large-scale, high-stakes testing on schools and classrooms and the adults and students who teach and learn in these environments.

THE IMPORTANCE OF THE EFFECTS OF TESTING

There are a number of reasons to be concerned about the consequences of testing on schools and classrooms, but two are particularly compelling:

- First, the goal of changing educational practice is one of the major justifications for implementing high-stakes tests. Advocates hope test scores will prompt schools to reform policy, encourage teachers to adopt more effective practices, and motivate students to work harder. Under these circumstances, the *Standards for Educational and Psychological Testing* make it clear that broad evidence about the consequences of testing is necessary for a thorough investigation of test validity (American Educational Research Association et al., 1999). Information about the broad impact of tests on the educational system is necessary when the purported benefits of tests include behavioral changes such as improved instruction or increased student motivation. Therefore, we need to examine whether these changes are occurring to ascertain whether high-stakes testing is meeting policymakers' goals for reform.

- Second, changes in behavior may, in turn, affect the validity of various interpretations of test scores. For example, some reactions to high-stakes tests, such as changes in the conditions under which tests are administered, will affect the relationship between test scores and achievement. These behaviors can lead to increases in scores without concomitant increases in knowledge—i.e., score inflation—which was discussed in Chapter Three. Without monitoring such changes in behavior, we will not know the extent to which gains in scores are due to real improvement in achievement rather than differences in testing conditions or other factors.

The Effects of Testing and Test Validity

It is worth making a brief detour at this point to explain why information about changes in school and classroom practices is important in judging the validity of test scores. As we have discussed, large-scale tests measure an extremely limited sample of behaviors—only a few questions are asked and they are limited to those that can fit into a few formats. People who use test scores—from policymakers to parents—do so in the hope that performance on the test questions is indicative of performance in a broader domain, such as third-grade language arts or first-year algebra. Under appropriate conditions, well-developed tests will support inferences from test scores to broader domains such as these.

However, certain practices can reduce the meaningfulness of test scores as indicators that students have mastered large subject-matter domains. For example, if the same test form is used repeatedly, teachers may become familiar with the specific items that appear on that form. If the test content becomes well known, teachers may shift their instruction accordingly. Such targeted teaching to those skills that are represented on a test can raise scores without increasing mastery of the broader domain. Although it is quite likely that students who learn the full curriculum will do well on a test that is sampled from that curriculum, the converse is not necessarily true. Students who do well on specific test questions that have been emphasized in their class may not have mastered the full curriculum. If this situation occurs, then the use one makes of the test score information—judging program quality, retaining students in grade, rewarding schools, and other such decisions—will be suspect.

Broadened Use of High-Stakes Testing to Promote Changes in School Practice

As we described in Chapter Two, there was little concern about the effects of testing on teaching prior to the 1970s. The federal government and the states used large-scale tests to monitor the status of the educational system and provide information that might be helpful to teachers and students. However, specific rewards or sanctions were seldom associated with performance. For example, the National Assessment of Educational Progress (NAEP), which is the only large-scale federally commissioned achievement test, was designed solely with a monitoring role in mind. William Bennett, former U.S. Secretary of Education, described this role as "supplying the American people with prompt, reliable, and comprehensive data on the educational performance of our children" (National Assessment of Educational Progress, 1987, 3). He likened NAEP to a measuring tool: "It is the closest thing we have to a barometer of our educational performance . . . as a nation . . ." When tests are conceived in this manner by policymakers, there is little concern about their direct impact on practice.

Beginning with the minimum competency testing movement in the 1970s, policymakers began to use test results in new ways—specifically, as the basis for decisions about individual performance. Tests grew more common in the 1980s, and the rationale for large-scale testing expanded from judging performance to influencing practice (Popham, 1987). With the advent of formal accountability systems in the 1990s, policymakers embraced a new, more potent vision for the role of assessment. They envisioned tests (often in combination with standards) as a mechanism to influence changes in practice, something that could be used "to exert a strong positive effect on schooling . . ." (Achieve, Inc., 2000, 2). Testing programs built in this mold provide incentives and/or sanctions for individual students (e.g., graduation, retention-in-grade) and/or for schools (e.g., cash rewards, administrative review) on the basis of test scores. The incentives indicate that performance has become an important issue to policymakers.

Test-based accountability systems, such as those that provide incentives and sanctions for both students and schools, are designed to affect schooling in multiple ways. For example, the California Department of Education articulated five ways that high-stakes, standards-based reform would lead to positive school changes (California Department of Education, 1998, p. 4):

1. Signal important content to teachers so that they can improve instruction

2. Identify learning that is below what is expected of students, thus motivating students and parents to put more effort into school work

3. Raise public awareness and prompt citizens to bring pressure to bear on ineffective schools

4. Encourage greater parental involvement

5. Facilitate the targeting of resources to schools that are in trouble.

This list of positive outcomes is typical of the rationale that other states provide to justify their high-stakes testing programs to policymakers and the public.

GATHERING EVIDENCE ABOUT THE EFFECTS OF HIGH-STAKES TESTING

In light of the changes that occurred in the uses of large-scale testing in the 1980s and 1990s, researchers began to investigate teachers' reactions to external assessment. The initial research on the impact of large-scale testing was conducted in the 1980s and early 1990s. In the mid-1990s, states began to implement statewide, test-based accountability systems, prompting renewed interest in the effects of testing on the practice of teaching. Large-scale studies of test validity and the effects of testing were conducted in a number of states that implemented such accountability systems. Research on these issues continues to the present day.

The bulk of the research on the effects of testing has been conducted using surveys and case studies. Typical of the survey research was a study conducted in 1991 by Shepard and Dougherty as part of a larger effort to examine the validity of test scores as well as the effects of testing on practice. The study was conducted in two large school districts with student populations in excess of 50,000. The researchers surveyed a sample of approximately 850 third-, fifth-, and sixth-grade teachers in approximately 100 schools. Surveys were administered in the spring, near the end of the school year. The surveys included questions about pressure to improve test scores, the effects on instruction, test preparation activities, controversial testing practices, use of the test results, and the effects—both positive and negative—of standardized testing.

More recently, the scope of survey research has been expanded to include statewide samples of teachers and principals, and the methods have expanded to include both written and telephone surveys. In the 1990s, researchers at RAND conducted a number of studies of state accountability systems, including those in Kentucky, Maryland, Vermont, and Washington. These studies usually included surveys of principals and teachers as well as quantitative analyses of test scores. For example, Koretz et al. (1996a) studied the effects of Kentucky's educational reform effort, which included a test-based accountability system that used portfolios of students' written work as well as more-traditional tests. A stratified random sample of 80 elementary schools and 98 middle schools was selected for the study. Both computer-assisted telephone interviews and written surveys were used to collect data. Representative samples of 186 fourth-grade teachers and 175 eighth-grade mathematics teachers were interviewed and surveyed. In addition, principals in the sampled schools were asked to participate in a telephone interview. The interviews with the principals focused on general support for the reform effort, the principals' own responses to the reform, the effects of the reform on their schools, how the test scores are used, and the burdens imposed by the testing program. Teachers were questioned on some of the same issues and also on test preparation, instructional practices, and their understanding of the testing program, particularly the portfolio component. Similar methods were used in the other states studied by the RAND researchers.

Case studies have also been used to examine the effects of high-stakes testing on practice. In a study published in 1991, Smith et al. conducted detailed observations of teachers in two Arizona elementary schools whose students took tests that had significant consequences. During the fall 1987 semester, the authors conducted daylong observations in 29 classrooms. Lessons were also audiotaped. The researchers also observed and recorded staff meetings. In January 1988, they selected a subset of 20 teachers for detailed open-ended interviews covering the validity of the tests, the effects of the tests on teachers, test preparation methods, and the effects of the tests on pupils. Subsequently, six teachers were selected for more-extensive observations occurring one, two, or three days a week during the spring of that year. In total, the six classes were observed for 81 days. The purpose of the observations was to understand "ordinary instruction"; therefore, the observers focused on what was taught, the methods used, the allocation of time, language and interaction among teachers and pupils, teaching materials, and classroom interruptions. The researchers used a variety of techniques to review and summarize the data and compare the situation in these classrooms to the literature on testing and its effects.

Other researchers have used case study techniques to study teaching practices within the context of high-stakes testing. McNeil and Valenzuela (2000) accumulated information from hundreds of Texas teachers and administrators over a period of a decade while the state implemented a test-based accountability system. Their research included in-depth longitudinal studies in three high schools as well as many years of professional development work with hundreds of teachers and dozens of principals and administrators. Borko and Elliott (1999) and Wolf and McIver (1999) focused their case studies of testing effects in a slightly different direction. They identified six "exemplary" elementary and middle schools in Kentucky (and later in Washington State) and conducted observations and interviews to see how the most respected administrators and teachers were reacting to testing mandates.

THE POSITIVE AND NEGATIVE EFFECTS OF HIGH-STAKES TESTING

The earlier discussion suggests that researchers need to cast a wide net when examining responses to large-scale, high-stakes testing programs because the developers of those programs envision them operating through many different mechanisms. On the positive side, one might expect to find changes in school policies that are designed to make schools more effective, changes in teaching practice that will enhance student achievement, and changes that result in increased motivation on the part of students. However, one might also find changes that most would consider negative, such as narrowing of the curriculum to tested topics to the exclusion of other domains of learning, inappropriate test preparation, or even cheating. Table 4.1 provides a partial list of the potential effects of high-stakes tests on students, teachers, administrators, and policymakers, differentiating between those effects that would be considered positive and those that would be considered negative.

Two issues complicate the problem of judging the net effect of large-scale, high-stakes testing:

- Many of the effects suggested by Table 4.1 are difficult to measure. For example, it is difficult to assess psychological variables such as motivation or competitiveness with any accuracy. Similarly, it is difficult to track the influence of diverse factors on policymaking. Furthermore, while it is possible to measure the quantity of many of the potential effects of high-stakes testing (e.g., how many hours were spent teaching decimal place values?), measuring the quality of those effects can be vexingly difficult (e.g., how well were place-value lessons taught?). As a result,

Table 4.1

Potential Effects of High-Stakes Testing

Positive Effects	Negative Effects
Effects on Students	
Provide students with better information about their own knowledge and skills	Frustrate students and discourage them from trying
Motivate students to work harder in school	Make students more competitive
Send clearer signals to students about what to study	Cause students to devalue grades and school assessments
Help students associate personal effort with rewards	
Effects on Teachers	
Support better diagnosis of individual student needs	Encourage teachers to focus more on specific test content than on curriculum standards
Help teachers identify areas of strength and weakness in their curriculum	Lead teachers to engage in inappropriate test preparation
Help teachers identify content not mastered by students and redirect instruction	Devalue teachers' sense of professional worth
Motivate teachers to work harder and smarter	Entice teachers to cheat when preparing or administering tests
Lead teachers to align instruction with standards	
Encourage teachers to participate in professional development to improve instruction	
Effects on Administrators	
Cause administrators to examine school policies related to curriculum and instruction	Lead administrators to enact policies to increase test scores but not necessarily increase learning
Help administrators judge the quality of their programs	Cause administrators to reallocate resources to tested subjects at the expense of other subjects
Lead administrators to change school policies to improve curriculum or instruction	Lead administrators to waste resources on test preparation
Help administrators make better resource allocation decisions, e.g., provide professional development	Distract administrators from other school needs and problems

Table 4.1—Continued

Positive Effects	Negative Effects
Effects on Policymakers	
Help policymakers to judge the effectiveness of educational policies	Provide misleading information that leads policymakers to suboptimum decisions
Improve policymakers' ability to monitor school system performance	Foster a "blame the victims" spirit among policymakers
Foster better allocation of state educational resources	Encourage a simplistic view of education and its goals

few of these potential consequences have been studied systematically. Research primarily focuses on school and classroom practices using teacher and principal surveys to gather information.

- The effects that are measurable are not measured in a common metric. For example, the amount of additional professional development teachers receive might be measured in hours, but relaxation of test administration rules to benefit students would have to be measured in some other way. As a result, there is no way to combine positive and negative effects to produce a "net" judgment about impact.

To make sense of the research on the effects of high-stakes testing on practice, it is helpful to differentiate among responses to high-stakes testing at different levels of the educational system. Most of the research has been conducted at the classroom level, and it has focused on changes in curriculum and instruction under the control of teachers. There is also some evidence about changes at the school level, including decisions about curriculum emphasis, teacher support, and programmatic changes. Less is known about the use of high-stakes test results by state policymakers.

Teacher Response to High-Stakes Testing

It is also helpful to differentiate among types of responses to high-stakes testing. Koretz, McCaffrey, and Hamilton (2001) identify seven categories of teacher responses to high-stakes tests and their likely effects on test scores and student learning (see Figure 4.1). They differentiate between three types of teacher responses: those that are positive (i.e., they have beneficial effects on learning and lead to valid

RAND *MR1554-4.1*

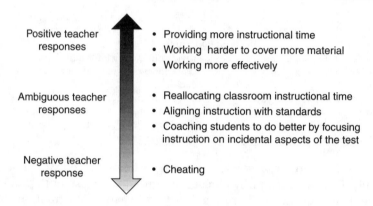

Positive teacher responses
- Providing more instructional time
- Working harder to cover more material
- Working more effectively

Ambiguous teacher responses
- Reallocating classroom instructional time
- Aligning instruction with standards
- Coaching students to do better by focusing instruction on incidental aspects of the test

Negative teacher response
- Cheating

Figure 4.1—Seven Categories of Teacher Responses to High-Stakes Testing

increases in scores), those that are negative (i.e., they lead to distortions of learning or inflated scores), and those whose impact is ambiguous (i.e., they can be positive or negative depending on the specific circumstances).

Some forms of teacher response, if handled effectively, are clearly positive: providing more instructional time, working harder to cover more material in a given amount of instructional time, and working more effectively by adopting a better curriculum or more-effective teaching methods. These are precisely the effects that proponents of high-stakes testing hope will occur. All of these effects have been documented to some extent by researchers, and all should generate real increases in student achievement.

Other forms of teacher response to high-stakes testing have ambiguous effects—that is, they can lead to real gains in student understanding and achievement or to inflation of scores (i.e., gains that do not generalize to other measures) or both, depending on the specific ways those gains are realized. Ambiguous responses include reallocating classroom instruction among topics or subjects to emphasize tested content instead of content that receives little or no emphasis on the test; aligning instruction with standards, which is a special case of curriculum reallocation motivated by attention to curriculum standards; and coaching students to do better on a test by focusing instruction on aspects of the test that are partly or entirely incidental to the definition of the domain the test is intended to represent.

Reallocation of instruction, alignment of instruction with test content, and coaching can be classified as positive effects when they focus on important aspects of the domain the test is designed to measure or specific skills that help students demonstrate their actual achievement. Those effects will be negative when they focus on specific features of test content or format that are not broadly reflective of the domain. For example, reallocation of classroom time to emphasize topics covered by the test can be beneficial if the coverage that was reduced or eliminated is on topics that are clearly less important than those given added emphasis. Conversely, reallocation can be negative if classroom time is taken away from important aspects of the domain that do not happen to be represented in the test (for example, because they are difficult to assess in a multiple-choice format).

Similarly, efforts to improve alignment can lead to a focusing of instruction that may either be beneficial or lead to inflation of test scores. If teachers focus more intently on desired outcomes at the expense of relatively unimportant material and do so effectively, the result should be higher achievement in terms of the desired outcomes and higher scores. On the other hand, if the material being de-emphasized as a result of this refocusing is important, scores may become inflated. The extent to which greater alignment—that is, sharper focus—or any other reallocation produces real gains in total achievement rather than score inflation depends in part on what goes *out of* focus as well as what *comes into* focus. The issue is further complicated because reasonable people may differ in their judgment about the relative merits of the topics that are emphasized or de-emphasized. For example, some may think that greater emphasis on spelling, grammar, and punctuation is appropriate while others may think that the time should be spent on other topics related to good writing, such as studying literary genres or learning to write for different audiences and different purposes.

A similar principle applies to coaching. Reasonable efforts to familiarize students with the format and other aspects of a test can increase the validity of scores. If students do not understand the test instructions or the question formats, or how they should record their answers, their scores will underestimate their actual learning. Removing these obstacles to performance by familiarizing students with the testing procedure makes their test results more valid. However, coaching can also inflate scores when it improves test performance by focusing on features of the test that are incidental to the domain the test is supposed to measure. Because these features are incidental, learning about them does not produce real improvements in students' knowledge of the domain.

A teacher can also respond to high-stakes testing by cheating, a response that is clearly negative and can only lead to inflation of scores.

Positive Classroom Effects

On the positive side, there is evidence that high-stakes tests have led teachers to work more effectively. Case studies revealed how high-stakes testing that includes innovative forms of assessment can encourage teachers to change their instructional practices in positive ways (Wolf and McIver, 1999; Borko and Elliott, 1999). They also reveal how some schools can seize on assessment requirements to rededicate themselves to quality (Wolf et al., 1999) and how testing programs can influence schools to refocus professional development and support services (Borko, Elliott, and Uchiyama, 1999). Bishop (1986) cites evidence from Ireland to support the contention that curriculum-based external examinations promote "the development of mentoring relationships between teachers and students." He also found that teachers in "all Regents" high schools in New York (schools that require all students to take demanding Regents courses in five core subjects) were inspired to work harder by their school's commitment to student success on the high-stakes Regents examination (Bishop and Mane, 1999).

States have also had some success using high-stakes tests as "instructional magnets" (Popham, 1987) to persuade teachers to reallocate instructional time to include new elements of the state curriculum. For example, both Vermont and Kentucky used test-based accountability systems as pivotal elements in large-scale curriculum reform efforts. Statewide surveys revealed that teachers in Vermont increased the amount of time they spent teaching problem-solving and mathematical representations to prepare students for the state's portfolio-based high-stakes assessment (Koretz et al., 1994). Similar survey results in Kentucky showed that the high-stakes, performance-based assessments in writing and mathematics strongly influenced teachers to make their instruction more consistent with the state curriculum in these areas (Stecher et al., 1998; Koretz et al., 1996a).

In addition, testing can provide useful information for curriculum and instructional decisionmaking. For instance, the majority of teachers in two high-stakes testing districts surveyed by Shepard and Dougherty (1991) said test results were helpful in identifying student strengths and weaknesses and in attracting additional resources for students with the greatest needs.

Neutral and Negative Classroom Effects

Despite these positive findings, a large share of the published research on the impact of high-stakes testing on educational practice describes neutral or deleterious effects.

Firestone, Mayrowetz, and Fairman (1998) found that high-stakes testing in Maryland and Maine had little effect on instructional practices one way or the other. Similarly, Jones et al. (1999) reported mixed effects of tests on teaching methods in North Carolina. For example, roughly equal percentages of teachers said they had either increased their use of inquiry projects (thought to have educational benefits but not necessarily useful in preparing students for the tests) or decreased their use. The same was true for the percentage of teachers who increased or decreased their amount of lecturing, use of textbooks, and use of worksheets.

Negative Curriculum Reallocation. In contrast, the evidence on negative reallocation of classroom instruction among certain topics or subjects is widespread. Researchers first began to notice that high-stakes tests led to negative reallocation in the late 1980s; the effect was described at the time as "narrowing" of the curriculum (Shepard and Dougherty, 1991). Moreover, the greater the stakes, the more likely that such narrowing would occur (Corbett and Wilson, 1991). For example, one of the first studies of the effects of testing (conducted in two Arizona schools in the late 1980s) showed reallocation among subjects that reduced the emphasis on important material. The study revealed that teachers neglected subjects such as science, social studies, and writing that were not part of the mandated testing program (Smith et al., 1991). Similar declines in instructional time for nontested subjects have been observed in statewide studies in other states including Maryland, North Carolina, and Washington (Koretz et al., 1996b; Jones et al., 1999; Stecher et al., 2000a). Figure 4.2 shows the shifts in instructional emphasis reported by fourth-grade teachers in Washington State, which has high-stakes testing in four of the eight subjects covered by state standards.

Research in Kentucky shows that the size of subject-to-subject shifts in emphasis can be substantial. Table 4.2 shows the average number of hours per week that fourth- and fifth-grade Kentucky teachers spent on seven different subjects. What makes the table interesting is that Kentucky tested some subjects in fourth grade and others in fifth

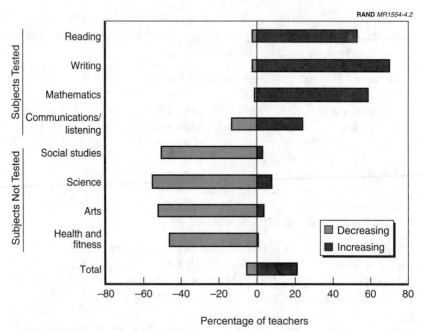

SOURCE: Stecher et al., 2000a, 21.

Figure 4.2—Percentage of Teachers Increasing or Decreasing Instructional Time in Tested and Nontested Subjects

Table 4.2

Mean Weekly Classroom Hours per Subject, Self-Contained Kentucky Fourth-Grade and Fifth-Grade Classrooms

	Fourth Grade	Fifth Grade
Subjects tested in fourth grade		
Reading	5.2	4.7
Writing**	5.8	4.0
Science**	5.2	3.5
Subjects tested in fifth grade		
Mathematics**	4.9	6.4
Social studies**	3.5	5.6
Arts and humanities**	1.5	2.4
Practical living/vocational education**	1.4	2.4

Note: **Significant at p<0.01.
SOURCE: Stecher and Barron, 1999.

grade. Teachers responded accordingly, leading to between-grade differences of an hour and a half per week or more in student exposure to subject content. Reallocating instructional time across grades to better align the available time with the subjects that are tested in each grade runs the risk of inflating scores on a grade-by-grade basis.

Negative reallocation can also occur within a subject area when teachers change their emphasis on specific topics in response to a test. Early research found that teachers tend to change course objectives and the sequence of the curriculum to correspond to the content and timing of new tests (Corbett and Wilson, 1988; Herman and Golan, [n.d.]; Darling-Hammond and Wise, 1985). Teachers also place more emphasis on topics that appear on the test and less emphasis on topics that are not tested.

For example, Romberg, Zarinia, and Williams (1989) surveyed a national representative sample of eighth-grade mathematics teachers and found that they increased coverage of basic skills, paper-and-pencil computation, and topics emphasized on their local tests while decreasing coverage of extended project work, work with calculators, and topics not emphasized on these tests. Shepard and Dougherty (1991) found that two-thirds to three-quarters of all teachers in two districts gave more emphasis to basic-skills instruction, vocabulary lists, word recognition skills and paper-and-pencil computation as a result of mandated tests that emphasized these topics.

Middle school teachers in Maryland and Maine also shifted their topic emphasis to correspond to the primary topic areas covered on the state test, although researchers reported that the extent of the change was not as dramatic as had been reported in other studies (Firestone, Mayrowetz, and Fairman, 1998). Opposite shifts were observed in Kentucky, where the testing program was designed to emphasize problem-solving in mathematics and extended writing in language arts. Teachers reduced their emphasis on computation and algorithms in mathematics and on the mechanics of writing (Koretz et al., 1996a). Researchers also found that pressure to improve test scores caused some Arizona teachers to neglect important curriculum elements that were not tested, including "reading real books, writing in authentic context, solving higher-order problems, creative and divergent thinking projects, longer-term integrative unit projects, [and] computer education" (Smith et al., 1991).

Adapting Teaching Styles to Test Formats. A more subtle type of negative reallocation—one that can shade into negative coaching— occurs when teachers adapt their teaching styles to make classroom presentations more like the format of the test or adopt instructional approaches that resemble testing methods.

For example, Shepard and Dougherty (1991) found that many teachers in two high-stakes testing districts were asking students to practice finding mistakes in written work rather than producing writing of their own. Smith and Rottenberg (1991) reported that teachers they studied in two Arizona schools had students solve only the type of math story problems that are found on the Iowa Test of Basic Skills (which was mandated in Arizona at the time). Stodolsky (1988) studied math and social studies instruction in 11 school districts in the Chicago area and found that high-stakes testing discouraged teachers from using joint- or team-teaching approaches and from changing their methods to facilitate serious student learning.

In Vermont, where the portfolio testing program encouraged teachers to include mathematical problem-solving in their curriculum, researchers found that many teachers focused narrowly on the aspects of problem-solving that would result in higher scores with the specific rubrics used in the tests rather than on problem-solving in the broadest sense (Stecher and Mitchell, 1995). This approach, which the authors labeled "rubric driven instruction," is an instance in which the distinction between substantively important and incidental aspects of the test is vague and the distinction between reallocation and coaching is blurred. If students' performance appears to improve when scored with one set of rubrics but does not appear to improve as much using another reasonable rubric, then scores may be inflated.

Negative Coaching. The literature contains other examples of negative coaching, i.e., activities that focus excessive amounts of time on incidental aspects of a test. For example, several studies have shown that "test preparation" activities (such as becoming familiar with the format of the test questions and learning how to record answers) can consume substantial amounts of limited instructional time. Herman and Golan (n.d.) surveyed upper-elementary schoolteachers in nine states and found that between one and four weeks of class time were diverted away from other learning activities and given to test preparation. Similar amounts of test preparation time (up to 100 hours per class) were reported in Arizona (Smith, 1994).

More recently, Jones et al. (1999) reported that 80 percent of teachers in North Carolina said their students spent more than 20 percent of their total instructional time practicing for end-of-grade tests. In these instances, the phrase "test preparation" was not clearly defined and exactly what activities occurred in preparing for the end-of-grade test is uncertain. However, this amount of coaching would certainly entail the loss of considerable learning time. In general, it is very difficult to quantify the extent of coaching without monitoring instruction for extended periods of time. An activity that uses a test-like format or representation may be quite appropriate in the short run, but the continuing use of such approaches to the exclusion of others constitutes coaching. In part because it is so difficult to detect, there is little research evidence about the extent of negative coaching. However, research on score inflation suggests that coaching is widespread in high-stakes testing situations.

Cheating. Cheating is the most extreme negative reaction to high-stakes testing. Cheating can take many forms: providing the actual test items in advance, providing hints during test administration, suggesting revisions, making changes to answer sheets before scoring, leaving pertinent materials in view during the testing session, and so on. Cheating scandals surface frequently. For example, in a recent case in New York City, investigators charged that dozens of teachers had cheated over a period of five years by giving students answers to the mathematics and reading tests that are used both as promotional gates and to rank schools. Educators told students which answers to change, had them put their initial answers on scrap paper and then corrected the students' answers before transferring them to the answer sheet, and gave them practice tests containing questions from the operational test (Goodnough, 1999).

Data on the incidence of cheating are scarce, but high-stakes testing can be expected to increase cheating. In a study of Kentucky educators' responses to the high-stakes Kentucky Instructional Results Information System (KIRIS) assessment, Koretz et al. (1996a) found that 36 percent of teachers reported seeing test questions rephrased during testing time either occasionally or frequently. Twenty-one percent reported seeing questions about content answered during testing time, and the same percentage reported seeing revisions recommended either during or after testing. Seventeen percent reported observing hints provided on correct answers. The corresponding percentages were somewhat lower in a parallel study of the lower-stakes Maryland School Performance Assessment Program (Koretz et al., 1996b).

School-Level Effects

Less is known about changes in policies at the district and school levels in response to high-stakes testing, but mixed evidence of some impact has appeared.

Positive Effects. Positive changes include revising district curriculum and testing programs to be consistent with state curricula and providing professional development opportunities for teachers (Stecher et al., 2000a). Bishop (1986) argues that external examination can also lead districts and schools to use their resources more effectively—for example, by hiring more qualified teachers and by providing essential instructional materials.

Testing programs can also be credited with helping focus resources on students or schools most in need. For example, about one-half of the principals in Washington State indicated that their school had added summer sessions in response to low test scores (Stecher and

Chun, 2001). Schools also reported adding after-school sessions and Saturday school to address the needs of low-performing students (Stecher et al., 2000a). State accountability systems can formalize this reallocation of resources based on test results. For example, California's accountability system provides additional financial resources as well as professional assistance to schools with low test scores to help them improve their effectiveness. Similarly, the new Elementary and Secondary Education Act (ESEA) legislation requires poor-performing schools to provide funds for tutoring for students whose test scores do not show adequate progress toward proficiency. Testing programs can also influence attitudes among staff; for example, they can promote greater cohesion, openness to new ideas, and esprit de corps, although these effects have only been documented anecdotally.

Negative Effects. On the other hand, researchers have also documented changes that appear to be designed to improve scores with little regard to their larger educational implications. For example, Koretz et al. (1996b) found that about one-third of principals in Maryland reassigned teachers among grades to improve the relative quality of teaching in the assessed grades. Because such shifts do not improve the quality of teaching across the grades, it is likely to inflate scores. Many Washington principals offered incentives to students in the form of parties and field trips for good test performance (Stecher et al., 2000a).

Other potential negative effects of high-stakes testing have recently come to the public's attention. Scores can be increased artificially, for example, by excluding low-scoring groups of students (e.g., students with disabilities, limited proficiency in English, or just low performance); by retaining low-scoring students in grades below those in which the test is administered; by allowing an increase in absences on test days; by granting waivers (exemptions from testing) demanded by parents; and by increasing dropout rates. Other potential effects would not inflate scores but could be important nevertheless. For example, Hauser, Pager, and Simmons (2000) argue that while current racial/ethnic differences in rates of retention in grade can be "almost entirely explained by social and economic deprivation among minority youth," group differences in test scores are larger than generally expected as a result of social and economic factors. Therefore, they suggest that tying promotion to test scores could increase racial/ethnic disparities in retention rates.

The extent to which these negative effects have occurred and the factors that may influence their occurrence remain uncertain, but there is a clear need for further monitoring of these effects and research on them. Although numerous news articles have addressed the negative effects of high-stakes testing, systematic research on the subject is limited. For example, a recent article in the Texas media argued that "schools that climbed in the state's accountability ratings in 1999 had substantially larger increases in TAAS [Texas Assessment of Academic Skills] exemptions for special education students than did other schools." However, the article also suggested that more investigation is needed to clarify the relationship between exclusions and accountability ratings (Dallas Morning News, 2000). Parent hostility to testing has led to increased requests for waivers for students to be exempted from testing in California and increased absences during the testing period (Neufeld, 2000).

Certainly, testing that creates "gates" through which students must pass in order to be promoted will lead to an increase in retention in grade, but it is unclear to what extent other forms of high-stakes testing will do the same. Grade retention has increased in Texas in recent years, particularly for African-American students (see, for example, Haney, 2000). The timing of this increase is not consistent with the implementation of the most recent high-stakes testing program in Texas (Carnoy, Loeb, and Smith, 2000), but it may be related to earlier waves of high-stakes testing in Texas. A study of the first years of Kentucky's high-stakes KIRIS assessment program found no evidence of increased retention in grade (Koretz and Barron, 1998).

Effects on Equity

It is important to note that while one of the rationales for test-based accountability is to improve educational equity, it is not clear that these accountability policies lead to more-equal educational opportunities or outcomes for students from different backgrounds. Indeed, some observers have argued that the negative effects of high-stakes testing on curriculum and instruction appear to be greater for low-performing students and low-scoring schools than they are for high-performing students or high-performing schools (Shepard, 1991).

Research regarding the effects of test-based accountability on equity is very limited. For example, McNeil (2000) reports that high-stakes testing in Texas is widening the gap between what is taught in historically low-performing schools (with predominantly minority and poor students) and what is taught in high-performing schools. Other observers have argued that the Texas system of statewide testing has improved the quality of instruction for students from all backgrounds. They point to the decreasing gap between racial/ethnic groups in their mean scores on the Texas state test (TAAS). However, recent evidence shows that the relative gains of Texas minority students on the TAAS were not echoed in the NAEP (an external, low-stakes test); the racial/ethnic gap in Texas did not narrow at all on the NAEP. This might reflect greater inflation of the scores of minority students (Klein et al., 2000) or artifacts of the testing program, such as "ceiling effects" that occur when a test is relatively easy for the students who are taking it, leading to an excessive number of students answering most questions correctly.

Another study showed that in Arizona, the amount of class time spent on test preparation and test administration was greater in urban, low-income, high-minority districts (Smith, 1997). Conversely, a high-stakes accountability system in Kentucky led some teachers to increase their academic expectations for students; however, more teachers reported increased expectations for high-achieving students than reported increased expectations for low-achieving or special education students as a result of the high-stakes tests (Koretz et al., 1996a).

SUMMARY

The net effect of high-stakes testing on policy and practice is uncertain. Researchers have not documented the desirable consequences of testing—providing more instruction, working harder, and working more effectively—as clearly as the undesirable ones—such as negative reallocation, negative alignment of classroom time to emphasize topics covered by a test, excessive coaching, and cheating. More important, researchers have not generally measured the extent or magnitude of the shifts in practice that they identified as a result of high-stakes testing.

Overall, the evidence suggests that large-scale high-stakes testing has been a relatively potent policy in terms of bringing about changes within schools and classrooms. Many of these changes appear to diminish students' exposure to curriculum, which undermines the meaning of the test scores. It will take more time and more research to determine on balance whether the positive impact on teaching practice and student learning outweigh the negative ones. Similarly, a new type of research will be needed to try to determine how to design accountability systems to maximize benefits and minimize negative consequences. In Chapter Six, we offer some recommendations for changing accountability systems to maximize the positive effects and minimize the negative consequences identified in this chapter.

Chapter Five

ACCOUNTABILITY AS SEEN THROUGH
A POLITICAL LENS

Lorraine M. McDonnell

- What political constituencies have an interest in the testing debate?

- How does public opinion influence elected officials?

- How are the actions of some policymakers at odds with standards of good testing practice?

To a large extent, recent federal and state educational assessment policies represent a political solution to an educational problem. Not only has the impetus for the movement toward large-scale achievement testing and test-based accountability systems come from politicians, the business community, and others outside the education establishment, but the definition of the problem to which they are the solution has a decidedly political cast to it. At the heart of the problem, as policymakers and others have defined it, is inadequate and unequal educational achievement: All students need to achieve at higher levels, particularly those who have been hampered by low expectations and insufficient opportunities to learn. But linked to this education-focused definition is a strong assumption that at least part of the problem can be attributed to the schools' lack of accountability to parents and other taxpayers who fund public education and give it legitimacy.

Consequently, standards and assessment policies embody both educational and political elements. The education portion of the solution focuses on the articulation of clear standards for academic content and student performance to guide teaching and learning and the alignment of classroom instruction with those standards. Testing is certainly part of the educational dimension of this policy; it provides a way to measure overall progress in meeting the standards and make instructional decisions about individual students. But testing is even more central to the political dimensions of the standards movement for which it primarily serves as an accountability mechanism. It is important, then, that we consider testing and accountability from a political as well as an educational perspective.

In this chapter, we elaborate on the idea that testing and accountability have become political issues. Then we describe the various constituencies that have an interest in educational assessment. We examine the political incentives that motivate policymakers and their constituents and how these incentives shape policy.[1] Finally, we discuss the implications of a political perspective on testing and whether political interests can be reconciled with the requirements for high-quality, fair, and accurate testing and with the concerns of professional educators.

Before proceeding, two caveats are in order:

- First, this chapter can only describe the issues that are raised when one looks at testing from a political perspective. Because of the lack of systematic studies on the topic, it does not evaluate the impact of politics on the design of the tests, or what happens when tests are used to advance policy or political purposes.

- Second, readers need to keep in mind that the implied claims by politicians that they can speak and act authoritatively on educational testing differ from similar claims made by educators or testing and measurement experts. In contrast to educators who speak with legitimacy derived from norms of professional prac-

---

[1] *Political incentive* is a widely used generic term that refers to those factors that motivate politicians, interest group representatives, and other citizens to act in the political arena. These motivations can include the desire of politicians to get re-elected, their interest in enacting particular kinds of policies, and interest groups' and citizens' interest in promoting specific policy goals. As with most domestic policy, the political incentives that motivate testing policy are diverse and vary over time and across political venues at the federal, state, and local levels.

tice, or testing and measurement experts who can draw upon both research and professional standards, politicians' claims to legitimacy come from their legal authority as elected representatives of the citizenry that funds public schools. The interests of politicians, educators, and testing and measurement experts may be given different weight depending on the circumstances, but all have sufficient legitimacy to be seriously considered. The design of testing policies will be more successful if efforts are made to reconcile these interests when they are at odds with one another.

STANDARDIZED TESTING FACILITATES POLITICAL OVERSIGHT OF EDUCATION

The idea that testing is useful for accountability purposes is based on the following assumptions:

- As public institutions, schools should be held accountable to citizens and their elected representatives for their effective operation and especially for student learning.

- However, because educators know a lot more about what occurs in schools than do either politicians or the public, this serious information asymmetry has often hindered efforts to hold schools accountable.

- Consequently, some kind of externally imposed, standardized instrument is needed to provide comparable data on schools and students, so as to equalize the information available to everyone with a stake in the educational system.

Thus, standardized testing has come to play a prominent role in the political oversight of public education.

Standardized tests are used in two different ways that represent fundamentally different perspectives on how they can serve as instruments of public accountability. For uses that have come to be called "low stakes," no significant, tangible, or direct consequences are attached to the assessment results. They are used to provide information about student achievement to students, parents, educators, and the public with the assumption that information alone is a sufficient incentive for these various groups to take action to improve the quality of schooling. It is also assumed that a standardized test can reliably and validly measure student achievement; that politicians, educators, parents, and the public will then act on the information generated by the test; and that their actions will improve educational quality and student achievement.

The "high-stakes" uses of tests, in contrast, are based on the assumption that information alone is insufficient to motivate educators to teach well and students to learn to high standards. Instead, the promise of rewards or the threat of sanctions is needed to ensure change. Rewards in the form of monetary bonuses may be given to schools or teachers. Sanctions may be imposed through external oversight or takeover by higher-level officials. For individual students, their test scores may play a part in decisions about promotion and graduation (Heubert and Hauser, 1999).

Holding educators and their students accountable for student performance is not the only way in which testing can be used as an accountability mechanism. Theories of democratic accountability also assume that citizens can and should hold their elected officials accountable for the performance of public schools (Gruber, 1987). Hence, voters may factor in educational quality when they judge the past performance of their elected officials.

Standards and assessment are also political issues because they require judgments about values and thus touch on the philosophical and cultural debates that are at the heart of politics. The promulgation of academic standards requires that state and local governments make choices about what is most important for students to learn and what constitutes mastery of that knowledge. Testing as part of an accountability system raises the difficult issue of "who should be held accountable to whom for what." This question can be answered only by taking a normative stand on the appropriate role of different governmental units and even on the role of the family versus that of the state.

WHICH GROUPS ARE INTERESTED IN TESTING AND ASSESSMENT?

In looking across the landscape of constituencies with an interest in educational testing, we can make these observations:

- The groups are numerous and diverse.

- Groups with similar purposes and constituents do not always hold comparable positions on testing issues.

- Student testing has become a highly visible issue, characterized by politics similar to those of other high-profile policies.

The groups that have an interest in testing range from well-organized national organizations such as the Business Roundtable and the National Education Association to small local groups such as Parents Against Proficiency Testing in Ohio and the Parents Coalition to Stop High Stakes Testing in New York. In between are organizations that represent elected officials, test publishers, school administrators, education researchers, students with special needs, and those pressing for equal learning opportunities for all students.

These groups all subscribe to the same general goal of improving student learning, but they disagree about the means to achieve it and the role of testing in education reform strategies. In most cases, a group's position on test-related issues is motivated by its material interests (whether or not group members stand to gain financially or could be sanctioned as a result of a particular test, for example) and by its beliefs about the proper role of testing. Group members may believe that testing is one of the few ways to ensure that the education system takes responsibility for poor students or, alternatively, they may believe that other measures of student learning are more reliable and valid.

Not only do groups with similar purposes and constituents not always hold comparable positions on testing issues, but their positions can also shift, depending on the particular issue. For example, both the American Federation of Teachers (AFT) and the National Education Association (NEA) have argued strongly in favor of using other indicators in addition to a single test score in making high-stakes decisions about individual students. However, the AFT has been more supportive of the high-stakes use of tests in making promotion and graduation decisions than the NEA. The NEA recently voted to support any legislation that allows parents to opt their children out of standardized testing requirements (Heubert and Hauser, 1999; Teachers vote to let parents decide on tests, 2001).

Similarly, a number of civil rights organizations, such as the National Association for the Advancement of Colored People (NAACP) and the Mexican-American Legal Defense and Educational Fund, have strongly opposed the high-stakes use of standardized tests, especially when they are the sole criterion in making decisions about students' promotion and graduation. In contrast, the Education Trust, an organization that promotes high standards for disadvantaged students, supports increased testing as part of a strategy to close the achievement gap between affluent and poor students and between white students and students of color.

A group's position on testing can shift depending on the specifics of the testing policy. For example, some governors and other state officials were opposed to the annual testing provisions that are part of the recent reauthorization of the 2001 Elementary and Secondary Education Act (ESEA). Their opposition stemmed from a belief that such a federal requirement would encroach on states' own prerogatives and on local control, and from their concerns about the cost of the testing and the disruption to the testing arrangements that states already have in place (Wilgoren, 2001). State officials were also apprehensive about what the political ramifications would be if the federally mandated tests were to show that many schools were making inadequate progress in improving student achievement (Lemann, 2001). Yet, many of these same officials have been at the forefront of state initiatives to require the local districts to use tests and to impose consequences on schools and students based on test scores.

Student testing has become a highly visible issue, characterized by a politics similar to that of other high-profile policies. The lobbying strategies and efforts to shape public opinion that are often employed by large interest groups are now being applied to testing issues. For example, the Massachusetts Teachers Association has been waging a major public relations campaign against the state's use of the Massachusetts Comprehensive Assessment System (MCAS) as a graduation requirement; that effort included a vivid television commercial urging viewers to "Say No to the MCAS Graduation Requirement" (Gehring, 2000; McFarlane, 2001). Similarly, as the ESEA reauthorization moved to conference committee, most of the organizations representing the education establishment, such as the teacher unions, the school administrator organization, and the school boards association, mobilized to press for modifications in the testing provisions that could adversely affect their members (Brownstein, 2001a). On the other side of the issue, the Business Roundtable, a strong supporter of standards and assessments, recently issued a booklet designed to assist its members and other advocates in addressing this "testing backlash"; i.e., the effort to minimize or eliminate high-stakes testing (Business Roundtable, 2001a).

But not all the politics of testing has revolved around the lobbying strategies of national organizations. Much of the testing backlash has been the result of grassroots organizing by suburban, middle-class parents. Examples include the recent boycott of New York's eighth-grade test organized by a group of mothers at a Scarsdale middle school (Zernike, 2001), the anti-MCAS petition drive organized by parents in six suburban legislative districts in Massachusetts (Greenberger, 2000), and a variety of rallies recently held in about a dozen states with the number of participants ranging from a dozen in Detroit to 1,500 in Albany (Manzo, 2001). The reasons that parents oppose the tests vary. They are concerned that extensive test preparation is hindering classroom innovation and that the standards being tested are vague or inappropriate. They are concerned that the tests put children who either have not had the opportunity to learn the material being tested or are poor test-takers at a disadvantage. And they are concerned that the tests consume too much time and put too much stress on younger students (Schrag, 2000).

It is too early to tell whether these grassroots protest activities will spread and come to represent a national movement in opposition to the high-stakes use of tests. At this point, however, the backlash is limited to suburban communities within a few states. Somewhat ironically, the parents of those students who are least likely to feel the adverse effects of high-stakes testing (suburban, upper-middle-class, white students) are the ones who have organized thus far. Whether they will be successful in mobilizing a broad spectrum of parents and the public will largely depend on how urban, minority, and working-class parents react if and when sanctions are imposed on large numbers of their children.[2]

WHAT FACTORS INFLUENCE TESTING POLICY?

Elected officials' interest in testing is typically motivated by genuine concern about students and their educational achievement. However, the electoral incentive plays a large role in that motivation, not only because of politicians' self-interest in getting re-elected, but also because they cannot accomplish their policy goals unless they are returned to office. The relationship between the politics of testing and electoral politics is especially close in those cases in which politicians such as George W. Bush have made student testing a centerpiece of their policy agendas, or have staked their re-election on raising student test scores as the governors of California and Georgia have done.[3] Politicians understandably prefer policies that are responsive to public opinion, produce at least some effects quickly, and have the potential for accomplishing purposes only tangentially related to testing (Downs, 1957; Kingdon, 1993; Moe, 2000).

Public Opinion

Because it can be volatile and not well informed on some issues, public opinion, as measured by surveys, does not always provide a clear and unambiguous measure of public sentiment. In addition,

---

[2]Much of the media's attention to the politics of testing has focused on lobbying aimed at the executive and legislative branches of the federal and state governments. However, civil rights groups in several states have also tried to use the courts to stop or modify high-stakes testing programs. Thus far, all of these attempts have been unsuccessful. The most notable was the GI Forum case in Texas in which the federal district court ruled that although the Texas Assessment of Academic Skills (TAAS) had a disparate impact on minority students, the test and its uses are not unconstitutional, and that the plaintiffs failed to prove that the disparate impact was more significant than the concomitant positive impact (GI Forum et al. v. Texas Education Agency et al., 87 F. Supp. 2d 667, W.D. Tex. 2000).

[3]Even if politicians do not choose to tie their re-election directly to student test scores, the policy may still be politicized simply because it can serve as a focal point for debates about what should be taught and tested and how test score data should be used. Test policy may also serve as a rallying point for interest group activity, and more indirectly, as a basis for citizens' decisions about whether to support the schools in matters such as bond elections.

politicians typically use public opinion polls as only one basis for making decisions, weighing them against their own policy preferences and those of constituency groups already mobilized around an issue. Nevertheless, public opinion can play an important legitimating function either in support of or in opposition to particular policy choices. Public opinion has been a source of diffuse support for those committed to an activist policy stance on testing, either for or against.

A variety of poll data indicate strong, stable support for standardized testing and its high-stakes uses, with the public also seeming to acknowledge its shortcomings. At the same time, responses to some survey items suggest that the public may not be particularly well informed about some aspects of student testing. Across a variety of state and national polls, 60 to 80 percent of respondents support the high-stakes use of tests (Johnson and Immerwahr, 1994; Elam and Rose, 1995; Mass Insight, 1997; Fuller, Hayward, and Kirst, 1998; Immerwahr, 1997). In the 1995 Phi Delta Kappan/Gallup poll, 65 percent of the respondents supported requiring students in their local communities to pass standardized tests for promotion from one grade to another, a proportion that has remained constant over the four times since 1978 that the question has been asked (Hochschild and Scott, 1998). A nationally representative survey of parents, conducted by Public Agenda in 2000, several months after the first reports of a parental testing backlash, obtained much the same results as earlier polls. Only 11 percent of those surveyed thought that their children were required to take too many standardized tests, and 67 percent strongly agreed with policies that impose higher academic standards even if they mean that their own children have to attend summer school before being promoted to the next grade (Public Agenda, 2000).[4]

There is also some evidence that the public understands the limitations of testing. For example, in the National Public Radio/Kaiser Family Foundation/Kennedy School national poll released in September 1999, 69 percent of those polled said that standardized

---

[4]An additional 19 percent of the sample said that they somewhat approved of such a policy even if their child has to attend summer school. When asked if they approved of the policy even if their child were held back in grade, 46 percent strongly approved and an additional 21 percent approved somewhat.

tests should be used to determine whether students are promoted or graduate (with no differences between parents and nonparents). But only 12 percent said that they were "very confident" that "test scores on standardized tests are an accurate indicator of a student's progress and abilities," although an additional 56 percent said that they were "somewhat confident" (NPR Online, 1999).

More-recent polls also suggest that the admonitions of testing experts and various professional groups about the dangers of decisions based on a single test score have filtered through to the public. In the 2000 Phi Delta Kappan/Gallup poll, only 13 percent of those surveyed believe that a single standardized test is the best way to measure student achievement, with 85 percent saying that standardized tests should be combined with either a teacher-designed test or a portfolio of student work (Rose and Gallup, 2000). Similarly, 79 percent of the parents surveyed by Public Agenda strongly or somewhat agreed with the statement, "it's wrong to use the results of just one test to decide whether a student gets promoted or graduates" (Public Agenda, 2000).

Looking across all the available poll data collected over the past two decades on public attitudes toward standardized testing, it appears that the public is more broadly supportive of high-stakes testing than are the interest groups that have taken a position on the topic. But there is also evidence that the public may not be particularly well informed on this and other education policy issues. We know, for example, that on general knowledge questions about education policy, public perceptions are often mistaken.[5] With regard to testing, 51 percent of the parents surveyed in the Public Agenda poll reported that they did not know whether the standardized tests that their children take ask fair questions that students should be able to answer (Public Agenda, 2000). It is important to note that for this item, parents' lack of knowledge is at least partly due to test security proce-

---

[5]For example, the 1996 Phi Delta Kappan/Gallup poll found that although the high school dropout rate has steadily declined, 64 percent of those surveyed thought that it had increased over the past 25 years. In the same survey, only 26 percent could accurately estimate the proportion of students receiving special education services (Elam, Rose, and Gallup, 1996). In a more recent Washington Post/Kaiser Family Foundation/Harvard University poll, only 29 percent of the registered voters surveyed knew that the federal government provides less than a quarter of the funding for the nation's public schools (Washington Post, 2000).

dures that minimize public release of test items. However, it might be reasonable to assume that if parents are poorly informed about this question, they and other members of the public might also be unaware of the full range of consequences related to high-stakes testing and the limits on the information that tests can provide.

Nevertheless, public opinion continues to buttress support for those policymakers who wish to pursue high-stakes testing policies. In fact, given the opposition of many influential interest groups to the kind of high-stakes testing embodied in the ESEA reauthorization, public opinion may be a critical resource for those politicians of both major political parties who favor the expanded testing now required (Brownstein, 2001b). The public may only have a vague idea of what constitutes student testing, but public support may be sufficient to give these policymakers political cover as they support the testing required by the ESEA reauthorization, thereby pursuing an agenda opposed by key interest groups and factions within their own parties.

The Need to Show Results Quickly

Two- and four-year electoral cycles make it difficult for politicians to sell patience to an electorate that expects quick results. This constraint makes education reforms with testing at their core particularly appealing because they seemingly alter what happens in individual classrooms within a very short period.

Close to 30 years of research on policy implementation have shown that policymakers at the federal and state levels often cannot "mandate what matters" (McLaughlin, 1987, 172); i.e., they may be able to impose broad requirements from afar, but they cannot anticipate and mandate the conditions that facilitate real change from the inside out. For education policy, this limitation has meant that reforms designed to alter classroom instruction have had only a limited impact because few top-down mandates or incentives are sufficient on their own to overcome a lack of local will or capacity.

However, externally mandated assessments constitute the one top-down policy lever that seems consistently to change local behavior. Although the impact of such assessments varies depending on the type of test, the grade levels being tested, students' socioeconomic status, and the uses to which the test is put, a growing body of research indicates that school and classroom practices do change in response to these tests (e.g., Firestone, Mayrowetz, and Fairman, 1998; Stecher et al., 1998; Mehrens, 1998; Corbett and Wilson, 1991).

Clearly, the effects of mandated assessments have not always been beneficial for students or what policymakers intended. Nevertheless, given the limited array of strategies available to them, politicians have viewed standardized testing as too powerful a lever not to be used. From their perspective, assessment policies also produce results quickly because test scores typically rise during the first few years after a new test is introduced. The validity of such score gains has long been questioned by researchers (Koretz, McCaffrey, and Hamilton, 2001; Linn, 2000), but most policymakers remain convinced that something real occurs if only because the tests shine a public spotlight on educators who must then respond.

The desire to produce some results within the constraints of the electoral cycle does not necessarily mean that policymakers expect all or most of the effects of a testing policy to be generated quickly. For example, Kentucky's education reform legislation gives schools 20 years to move all their students to the "proficient" level of mastery of the state standards, and the ESEA reauthorization recently passed by the Congress gives schools 12 years to move all students to the "proficient" level, as defined by state standards. In these and similar cases, however, policymakers expect testing policies to produce steady, incremental progress, thus indicating to the public that schools are improving and moving in a direction consistent with the long-term goals of the policy.

The challenge for elected officials is being able to persuade their constituents that sufficient progress is being made to warrant their continued support of public education while at the same time modifying policies that are not working as intended or are producing negative consequences. Achieving such a balance is especially difficult if policymakers want to avoid adding additional tests and other policy requirements as part of their corrective action or abruptly changing policy direction when initial choices do not seem to be working. However, these two options often prevail over a "stay-the-course" approach because political candidates often have to distinguish themselves from their opponents by proposing new policies, or because they sense that the public is dissatisfied with the status quo and expects a change in direction.

TESTING AS A ROUTE TO ACHIEVING OTHER POLICY GOALS

In trying to balance competing constituent interests, elected officials may use testing policies to satisfy demands not directly related to the ostensible purposes of testing and assessment or to diffuse efforts to adopt controversial policies. For example, advocates for students with disabilities have lobbied federal and state officials to include them in standards and accountability systems as a way of requiring schools to be more explicitly and publicly accountable for those students (McDonnell, McLaughlin, and Morison, 1997). As a result, testing accommodations for students with disabilities have increased over the past few years, raising the question of whether or not those students' test scores should be "flagged" to indicate that they took the test under different conditions. Although this question is of interest to psychometricians and others concerned about valid interpretations of long-term trends in test score data, it is of considerably less significance to policymakers and special education interest groups who see the participation of students with disabilities in a state testing system to be of greater importance than whatever data are produced.

For policymakers who are concerned about preserving the vitality of the public school system in the face of moves to implement a voucher system, standards and assessment policies have become a way to show that public education can be rigorous, responsive, and accountable. In fact, one could argue that the standards and assessment movement is currently the only "big idea" serving as a counterpoint to vouchers. It is possible in the long term, however, that the failure of testing and accountability policies, as evidenced by a steady stream of low test scores or negative consequences imposed on many students, may increase public and elite support for vouchers and greater school choice.

In this section, we have explored how political imperatives can broaden the rationale for testing policies and expand the criteria by which their success is judged. The next section examines how those imperatives shape the purposes and uses to which standardized tests are put, and the extent to which the politics of testing places it at odds with professional testing standards.

THE INFLUENCE OF POLITICS ON HOW TESTS ARE USED

The discussion thus far has just alluded to the multiple purposes of testing. Interviews with officials and a review of current assessment policies indicate that policymakers expect testing to accomplish at least seven different types of purposes:

- Provide information about the status of the education system

- Aid in instructional decisions about individual students

- Bring greater curricular coherence to the system

- Motivate students to perform better and parents to demand higher performance

- Act as a lever to change instructional content and strategies

- Hold schools and educators accountable for student performance

- Certify individual students as having attained specified levels of achievement or mastery (McDonnell, 1994b; Heubert and Hauser, 1999).

The purposes underlying a particular assessment policy depend on the political history, culture, and ideology of the institutions enacting the policy. Assessment policies have also varied in their purpose and use as states have moved away from low-stakes tests that primarily served informational purposes to tests designed to hold schools and students accountable through the imposition of rewards and sanctions, change classroom instruction, and certify individual students for promotion and graduation.

The shift from low-stakes to high-stakes uses has also been accompanied by a move on the part of a growing number of states and some large urban school districts to use the same test for multiple purposes. So, for example, a state assessment tied to state curriculum standards might be used to provide information on the status of the system, influence classroom instruction in a particular direction, reward and sanction schools, and make decisions about student promotion and graduation.

In using the same test for multiple, high-stakes purposes, policymakers are at odds with the professional standards of the testing and measurement community. Among those standards are the need to base high-stakes decisions on more than a single test, validate tests for each separate intended use, and provide adequate resources for students to learn the content being tested (American Educational Research Association, 2000). In disregarding these standards, policymakers are using assessments in ways that exceed the limits of current testing technology. As a National Research Council report on high-stakes testing noted:

> . . . policy and public expectations of testing generally exceed the technological capacity of the tests themselves. One of the most common reasons for this gap is that policymakers, under constituent pressure to improve schools, often decide to use existing tests for purposes for which they were neither intended nor sufficiently validated. So, for example, tests designed to produce valid measures of performance only at the aggregate level—for schools and classrooms—are used to report on and make decisions about individual students. In such instances, serious consequences (such as retention in grade) may be unfairly imposed on individual students. That injustice is further compounded if the skills being tested do not reflect or validly measure what students have been taught (Heubert and Hauser, 1999, 30).

Although there are a number of reasons for this disjuncture between standards of good testing practice and policymakers' actions, three are especially notable:

• The first reason has already been mentioned: Policymakers often rely on existing tests because they perceive a fleeting political opportunity to act, thus necessitating that they move quickly while they have an open policy window. Or they may believe that, even with imperfect tests, more good than harm will result. Policymakers often acknowledge that critics of current testing systems are making valid points. However, from their perspective, the technical constraints identified by testing experts are problems that should be remedied to the largest extent possible, but in an iterative fashion simultaneous with the implementation of test-based policy (McDonnell, 1994b). Elected officials are people of action who cannot wait for the perfect test, and are willing to settle for one that is less than optimal on the assumption that it can be improved over time and that, in the interim, students will benefit from focused attention on their learning.

- Another reason for the disjuncture between standards of good testing practice and policymakers' actions is that policymakers, educators, and testing experts operate in very different worlds, and each group has only a limited understanding of the others' incentives, constraints, and day-to-day work. For many politicians, this lack of understanding means that they are crafting policies with limited knowledge of the nature of teaching and learning and of the role of tests in measuring teaching and learning. This limitation has been noted in a recent analysis of the debate over the ESEA reauthorization. Members of Congress with close ties to the education system or who themselves have been teachers are skeptical of how much can be accomplished with additional testing requirements. Those without firsthand experience in schools argue that it is critical to be able to measure what students are learning, and that annual tests are the way to do it and to achieve the ultimate goal of improving educational quality (Nather, 2001).

- Finally, the relatively low cost of the standardized tests and the low levels of investment that policymakers are willing to make in education reform have accelerated the use of the tests for multiple purposes and widened the rift between policy and standards of good testing practice. Although most assessment policies are part of larger reform strategies that include funding for student remediation, curriculum and test development, and teacher training, those funds are often insufficient to meet the demands of new testing and accountability systems.

Because the cost of the tests themselves is relatively low ($3 to $35 per student) and the tests seem to produce a lot of "bang for the buck," policymakers often underestimate the full costs of preparing teachers to convey the requisite curriculum effectively and of giving students adequate opportunities to learn it. The problem of underinvestment is compounded by the tight timelines under which these systems typically have to be implemented and show results. The potential effects of even reasonably adequate funding is likely to be diminished if the time frame is unreasonable. These funding and time pressures, then, work against the development of separate tests for different purposes.

Despite their desire to move quickly and to use tests that are readily available, policymakers have not been entirely unresponsive to the concerns of testing experts and educators. Whether in response to the criticisms of experts, the threat of lawsuits, or potential parental and teacher backlash, some states, for example, have delayed full implementation of high school exit exams or have lowered the score required to pass them. However, anyone surveying the current terrain of testing policy has to be struck by what appears to be a widespread resolve by politicians at the federal, state, and local levels to persist in their efforts to implement high-stakes testing and accountability systems.

RECONCILING POLICYMAKING IMPERATIVES WITH GOOD TESTING STANDARDS

Simply by virtue of the different worlds in which they work, a cultural divide will always exist between policymakers and the testing and measurement community. Even if that divide can never be bridged entirely, it can be narrowed. Yet over the past decade, the two communities seem to have moved farther apart in their views about student testing and its uses. Reconciling political imperatives with good testing standards requires that both policymakers and testing and measurement professionals change their actions and worldviews. In this conclusion, we describe how we believe they can move toward this reconciliation.

Recommendations for Policymakers

Policymakers need to consider the full costs of the testing systems they seek to implement. The most important of these costs results from the need to provide every student who is subject to high-stakes testing with adequate and appropriate opportunities to learn the content of the tests. A realistic assessment of the human resource, financial, and time investments necessary before most students can be reasonably expected to have mastered the requisite content will likely slow the current rate at which high-stakes testing is implemented.

Policymakers also need to persuade their constituents to be more patient in their judgments about public education. This applies especially to the two-thirds of voters who have no school-age children and little firsthand knowledge of schools. Persuading the public to be patient will require evidence that schools are, indeed, responsive to public expectations. However, another part of promoting patience on the part of the public is convincing citizens that accountability is a two-way street—schools cannot perform to community standards unless the community meets its obligations to adequately support the schools. Arguing against quick policy "fixes" is always difficult, but the success of some political leaders suggests that it can be done.

Above all, narrowing the gap between political imperatives and testing standards requires that policymakers are more accepting of the limitations of tests and their potential uses. Like many myths concerning public policy, the belief that assessments can provide unbiased and comprehensive data about student achievement is an influential one (De Neufville and Barton, 1987). Policymakers and their constituents want to believe that judgments about local schools and individual students are based on information that is technically sound and free of bias. These assumptions are even more critical when some schools and students are rewarded and others are sanctioned.

When policy creates winners and losers, policy decisions need to be justified on what appear to be objective grounds. Therefore, even if policymakers were to be more accepting of the limits of testing, they would still need to replace the myth of the objective test with an equally powerful one because "policymaking is about persuasion and myths persuade" (McDonnell, 1994a, 413). Whatever that replacement myth is, it will still have to serve the same public function—facilitating the political accountability of schools and allocating scarce resources in a seemingly fair and impartial way.

Recommendations for Testing and Measurement Professionals

Our recommendations for the testing and measurement community are primarily words of caution, identifying the shortcomings of current systems by noting what is not working and indicating where harmful or unintended consequences are likely to occur.

The role of the critic is an honorable and appropriate one for scholars, but the events of the past decade suggest that if testing experts want their admonitions to be heeded, they may have to change their strategies. Above all, they need to provide policymakers with alternatives to current testing regimes that are feasible and that address the public's desire for schools that are more accountable, responsive, and effective. Just as it will be difficult for policymakers to accept the limits of testing, it will be difficult for many members of the testing and measurement community to move from the role of critic to the role of system builder. Without compromising their own research-based principles, they will need to accept that, in a democracy, the authority for deciding the contours of a testing system rests with elected officials, and that accountability to the electorate is as legitimate a claim to authority as is scientific knowledge.

In the short term, the most effective strategy will probably be for testing experts to identify changes that can be made to the existing testing and accountability systems to make them reasonably consistent with standards of good testing practice. In doing this, they will need to take into account the political dimension. The tests must provide information about students and schools that is valid, comparable, and understandable to the public, and that can be used to leverage and motivate the behavior of both educators and students. And any system must produce tangible and credible results within a reasonable time frame.

None of these changes will be straightforward or easy to accomplish. However, one way to begin the process would be to combine the political and professional oversight of testing and assessment systems. Often in state systems, these functions are separate: Expert panels evaluate and advise on the technical aspects of a particular test, whereas decisions about its uses are made independently, often by state legislators. More closely integrating these two functions would allow each group to better understand the other's values and concerns and to deliberate about ways to accommodate their differing perspectives. If viewing testing through a political lens tells us anything, it is that political and professional perspectives must be reconciled if students are to benefit from the hopes and expectations of each group.

Chapter Six

IMPROVING TEST-BASED ACCOUNTABILITY

Laura S. Hamilton and Brian M. Stecher

- What do we know about test-based accountability systems?

- What are the steps we can take to improve the technical quality of tests?

- How can we ensure that teachers' classroom practices support the goals of assessment programs?

- How can we integrate the perspectives of both politicians and educators?

Test-based accountability has been a potent educational policy, and research suggests that it has had a large impact on school and classroom practice in just a short period of time. For example, the implementation of high-stakes testing has almost always led to increases in test scores. If these increases reflect improved learning, they provide *prima facie* evidence of the effectiveness of the policy for improving education. Moreover, in many cases, equal or even greater gains have been realized among low-performing students than among high-performing students, which suggests that test-based accountability may increase equity. It is extremely rare to find programs or policies for which this is true.

But the overall judgment about test-based accountability is not quite that simple. In some states, test score increases taper off after two or three years, and it is difficult to sustain growth thereafter. In addition, scores on other tests designed to measure similar content do not always give the same results as the high-stakes tests that are part of accountability systems. For a variety of reasons, students do not seem to do as well on other tests that are designed to measure the same things. So test-based accountability remains controversial because there is inadequate evidence to make clear judgments about its effectiveness in raising test scores and achieving its other goals.

One of the reasons for the lack of simple answers and unambiguous prescriptions about test-based accountability is that the goals of these systems, their specific features, and the conditions under which they are implemented vary from jurisdiction to jurisdiction. Many design decisions must derive from an understanding of the local context and the wishes and needs of the local stakeholders, and it is unlikely that a single model of accountability could be designed to fit every context.

Another source of complexity is the fact that accountability often requires trade-offs among competing values. For example, policymakers must balance the desire for more-reliable test scores (which derive from longer tests) against the concerns of teachers and parents that excessive classroom time is being consumed by testing. Similarly, the desire to hold all schools and students to a common standard typically results in the need to require larger test score gains among low-scoring schools than among high-scoring ones. This appears to many to contradict the commitment to equitable treatment of all students. Such tensions between competing desires were apparent throughout this book, whether we were discussing test use, test quality, testing effects, or the politics of testing.

At the present time, test-based accountability is a "work in progress" and there are still technical, operational, and political challenges to be overcome. Those states[1] that have already begun to implement test-based accountability systems have experienced a variety of problems as well as successes, and state policymakers and educators are looking for ways to improve those systems. Those states that will be developing accountability systems for the first time in response to requirements in the recent No Child Left Behind (NCLB) legislation

---

[1] In much of this discussion we refer to "states" as the units responsible for developing, implementing, and revising accountability systems, but the issues we discuss are equally applicable to other units including districts and the nation.

have a loose framework to follow, but policymakers and educators are looking for advice on all aspects of their systems.

Policymakers are keenly interested in ensuring that testing has positive effects on instruction and have instituted changes to address some of the concerns raised by researchers and others. For example, many states are implementing more-rigorous administrative controls to standardize testing conditions and the handling of testing materials to address concerns about security breaches. Similarly, federal policymakers responded to researchers' arguments about the need for an independent measure of achievement to validate the changes that occur in accountability tests by including National Assessment of Educational Progress (NAEP) testing as a requirement in NCLB.

So what do we recommend that policymakers do? Unfortunately, the complexity of the issues and the ambiguity of the existing research do not allow our recommendations to take the form of a practical "how-to" guide for policymakers and practitioners. Rather, in the following discussion, we alert policymakers to a variety of issues whose resolution will lead to accountability systems that are more likely to provide accurate and timely information to stakeholders while fostering higher-quality instruction for students. Although much of this advice relates to the design of accountability systems and is therefore targeted primarily to state policymakers, many of the issues we discuss are likely to be of interest to others who are involved with carrying out the provisions of accountability systems. At the end of this book, we list some additional resources, including a new set of accountability system standards developed by the Center for Research on Evaluation, Standards, and Student Testing (CRESST), the Consortium for Policy Research in Education, and the Education Commission of the States (Baker et al., 2002).

Our discussion is organized around the areas we discussed in previous chapters: technical quality, practice effects, and political considerations. The guidelines in each area are presented in Table 6.1 and elaborated on in the next sections.

Table 6.1

Guidelines for Improving Accountability Systems

Treat a Test-Based Accountability System as Dynamic and Flexible
Change test items regularly so that individual items do not become too familiar to teachers and test-takers
Consider major system upgrades to take advantage of new designs or enhancements when past practices become obsolete
Monitor and Improve Technical Quality
Conduct ongoing evaluation of technical quality to ensure that the systems continue to meet the needs of students, educators, policymakers, and the public
Incorporate multiple measures and multiple formats to reduce the risk of making incorrect decisions
Incorporate findings from cognitive psychology to ensure that tests reflect (1) the way students learn and demonstrate competence and (2) the system's instructional goals
Collect and maintain rich student-level data that allow tracking individual students over time
Adopt stable statistical indicators that reflect real differences in student achievement and minimize measurement and sampling errors
Design Systems That Have Positive Effects on Practice
Align teacher professional development and curriculum with standards and assessments so that teachers understand and support the system's goals and respond with effective classroom practices
Conduct ongoing research and evaluation of effects on practice to guide school reform efforts
Clarify the desired balance between accountability purposes and instructional purposes as a basis for making decisions among competing demands
Create incentives that promote desired goals, thus taking advantage of the strong response that high-stakes testing elicits from schools and teachers
Consider each policy's potential effects on equity to improve the performance and opportunities of students who have traditionally experienced low levels of academic success
Consider the Political Context
Facilitate integration of political and professional perspectives to remove obstructions to progress and build better tests and accountability systems
Incorporate parents' perspectives to make sure that accountability systems provide the information needed for more-effective parental involvement and decisionmaking
Explore costs and benefits of alternative approaches in order to make well-informed decisions

FIRST, SOME GENERAL ADVICE

We believe that an accountability system should be dynamic, not static; that is, it should be subject to ongoing review and revision. It is easy to understand why policymakers might fall into the trap of allowing a large-scale testing program to operate for years without modifications. Considerable effort is necessary to enact and implement an accountability system, and once the system is operational there is a natural tendency to move on to other matters. Furthermore, the desire to make scores comparable over time affords a strong rationale for leaving things as they are. Nevertheless, we believe that an accountability system needs regular maintenance and periodic upgrades. For example:

- Test items should be changed according to a regular cycle so individual questions do not become too familiar to teachers and test-takers.

- Major accountability system upgrades should be considered when new designs or enhancements make past practices obsolete. For example, item response theory (IRT)[2] permitted better test development and scoring for large-scale tests, and many testing programs have incorporated IRT models into their development process.

At the same time, accountability system upgrades should be done only when warranted and in a way that promotes coherence rather than confusion. Too-frequent changes in testing and accountability policies may lead to a system that provides inaccurate information and that leaves practitioners unsure about what the system's goals are. Our suggestions are based on what is currently known about test-based accountability and will undoubtedly need to be refined as new evidence accumulates.

---

[2] *Item response theory* is an approach to modeling the relationship between performance on a test item and proficiency on the underlying construct the test is designed to measure. IRT is commonly used to analyze and produce scores on large-scale tests.

IMPROVING TECHNICAL QUALITY

In this section, we present advice about ways to ensure adequate quality of information from test-based accountability systems. There is some overlap between issues that are relevant to technical quality and issues that are relevant to practice (which are discussed in the next section). For example, the use of multiple measures not only changes the quality of the information, but also provides a different set of incentives than when a single test form is used. It is less important how these issues are classified than that they are brought to the fore.

Conduct Ongoing Evaluation of Technical Quality

To ensure that an accountability system continues to meet the needs of students, educators, policymakers, and the public, it must include a monitoring function that provides periodic reports on how well the system is working. Regular assessments of technical quality should be conducted to examine the reliability and validity of student scores, school aggregate scores, student gains, and school gains. These assessments should go beyond the technical studies that are part of most existing programs. In particular, the inclusion of an audit mechanism can be a useful approach for evaluating the validity of scores and changes in scores over time. This would involve periodic administration of a test that is designed to measure constructs similar to those measured by the accountability tests but that does not resemble the accountability test too closely. The test should be one for which good technical quality has been demonstrated and that is judged to be sufficiently aligned with local or state standards.

There are a number of approaches to incorporating audit testing that would not require a great increase in testing time or costs. Because the audit test results would not be used for making decisions about students or schools, it may be feasible to administer the test to a sample of students, or to administer different parts of the test to different students. To make the best use of audit test results, efforts should be made to disseminate them broadly in ways that will enhance stakeholder understanding of the information they contain.

At the same time, it is important to recognize that there are no clear-cut rules regarding how an audit testing system should be designed or how differences in trends should be interpreted. Although we discussed some earlier work in which scores and trends on accountability tests and audit tests were compared, it is difficult to interpret these findings because we do not know what a reasonable level of discrepancy is. We would not expect to see perfect correspondence because of differences in the scope of coverage and the specific features of the items, but the existence of very large discrepancies raises concerns. Additional research is needed to identify the elements of performance on tests and how these elements map onto other tests, and to understand the nature of discrepancies among scores on different tests. A framework developed by Koretz, McCaffrey, and Hamilton (2001) provides a starting point for this work.

Research is also needed to understand what kinds of audit mechanisms are most effective. In particular, we need to determine how closely the audit test should resemble the accountability test in order to provide a valid measure without itself being susceptible to the factors that lead to score inflation on the accountability test.

Another part of the interpretive question is the need to gather information in other subject areas to portray a more complete picture of achievement. The scope of constructs that have been considered in research to date has been fairly narrow, focusing on the subjects that are part of the accountability systems that have been studied. Many legitimate instructional objectives have been ignored in the literature to date, even though critics of test-based accountability have expressed concern about the effects of those systems on subjects that are not tested.

Exploring ways in which these systems affect proficiency in the arts, acquisition of social skills, and even performance in the core academic subjects of science and social studies (particularly in states that do not include these subjects in their testing programs) would contribute to states' understanding of the effects of test-based accountability on student achievement. In states such as California, for example, where science and social studies are currently not tested until the ninth grade, administering achievement tests in these subjects to one or more elementary or middle school grades could provide important information regarding possible deleterious effects of reading and mathematics testing on achievement in nontested subjects. These results could then be used to help policymakers adjust the state's accountability policies where necessary.

Incorporate Multiple Measures and Multiple Formats

Although published standards for high-stakes testing make it clear that decisions about individuals or institutions should be based on multiple measures of performance (American Educational Research Association, 2000), there is no agreement about how to implement this standard. The purpose of the multiple-measures recommendation is to reduce the risk of making incorrect decisions due to the limitations of test scores, including measurement error. However, systems that do include more than a single test vary in the degree to which they are consistent with the spirit of the professional standards. For example, a system in which decisions are conjunctive (i.e., the student must pass every one of a set of tests) is less consistent with those standards than one that is compensatory (i.e., information is combined such that high performance on one test compensates for low performance on another) because in the former system a single low test score may result in a negative consequence for a student.

Furthermore, the use of multiple measures may improve the validity of the system by assessing a broader range of outcomes and reducing the likelihood of excessive narrowing of the curriculum. Although most states still rely on test scores alone rather than incorporating other information into accountability decisions, multiple measures can also include nontest information. In most states, improved data systems are needed before nontest indicators, such as graduation rates, can be included. States should continue to explore options for including nontest information, especially to the extent that such information reflects important goals or values of the public education system.

Alternatives to Single-Form Tests. States should also explore alternatives to the single-form test that is commonly used. At a minimum, states should change the items that are administered each year to avoid the most severe types of score inflation. A more ambitious option is matrix sampling of items to increase coverage and, perhaps, to enable multiple-item formats (e.g., multiple-choice, short-answer, essay) to be incorporated into the testing system. Some states already include short-answer and essay questions in their accountability testing, and others will be considering including such items as they seek to develop new tests that reflect their state standards.

Taking Advantage of Information Technology. Another option would take advantage of the increasing presence of information technology in schools and classrooms by administering computerized tests. As discussed in an earlier RAND report (Hamilton, Klein, and Lorie, 2000), computers make it possible to administer tests that are adaptive—i.e., adjusted to the proficiency level of the examinee—and that incorporate novel item formats that are not feasible or are overly costly in the absence of technology.

Computerized adaptive testing, or CAT, offers several advantages over current paper-and-pencil methods, including reduced testing time, enhanced security, and more rapid reporting of results. The adaptive nature of the tests, and the availability of a large pool of items, enable tests to be administered multiple times throughout the year, and facilitates measuring growth, accommodating assessment to individual student needs, and integrating assessment with instruction. Computers also offer an opportunity to revolutionize the way in which testing is done (Bennett, 1998). For example, multimedia technologies permit the inclusion of film and audio in addition to written artifacts in a history exam. A number of issues need to be addressed to ensure appropriate and fair implementation of computer-based assessment, but the time appears ripe for an exploration of technology's role in test-based accountability systems.

Incorporate Findings from Cognitive Psychology

There is increasing acknowledgment of the importance of developing tests that have good measurement properties but that also tap appropriate cognitive processes. While important for instructional feedback purposes, this may be even more critical in the context of test-based accountability systems that are intended to drive instruction. The National Research Council's Committee on the Foundations of Assessment, in its report *Knowing What Students Know* (2001), described three pillars on which assessments should rest: a model of how students represent knowledge and develop competence, tasks that allow one to observe students' performance, and an interpretation method for drawing inferences from these observations. The report argues that the first pillar—a model of learning—is insufficiently developed in most large-scale testing systems, and that most existing tests fail to measure several important aspects of learning, such as students' organization of knowledge or use of problem-solving strategies. This may arise in part from a long-standing schism between the fields of psychometrics and cognitive psychology, which has resulted in insufficient levels of collaboration among members of both fields (Glaser, 2001).

Assessment development should be guided by advances in both cognitive sciences and psychometric theory, and should be informed by input from cognitive researchers, testing experts, curriculum experts, educators, and policymakers. A model of learning should guide the development of both the test and the standards that communicate what students are supposed to accomplish. As states select measures for use in their accountability systems, they should keep these issues in mind and seek input from experts in cognitive psychology who can help them evaluate existing tests or develop new ones that are aligned with the kinds of instructional goals the system is intended to promote.

Part of states' ongoing evaluation efforts could include cognitive analyses of test items, using, for example, student interviews and think-aloud protocols (see Chapter Three). Such data could help test developers ensure that tests are tapping the kinds of skills and processes that they are intended to assess. Although taking these steps does not guarantee that tests measure what they are supposed to measure, they can provide important validity evidence to guide decisions and interpretation of results.

Collect and Maintain Rich Student-Level Data

Although most states administer tests that produce reliable scores for students, few states maintain the necessary data to track individual students' progress over time. By developing a data system that includes linked student-level data along with student and school characteristics, states would be able to address problems of student mobility. Such data also enable states to conduct analyses of achievement growth among different groups of students and would facilitate the kind of evaluative work discussed above. Although many states currently report results separately for subgroups of the student population, the lack of direct measures of growth sometimes makes them difficult to interpret.

States should also conduct ongoing analyses of the performance of groups whose members may not be numerous enough to permit separate reporting. English-language learners and students with disabilities are increasingly being included in high-stakes testing systems, and, as discussed in Chapter Three, little is currently known about the validity of scores for these groups. Data for these students should include information about their level of performance on previously administered tests as well as their level of performance in their instructional program, their specific disability classification (in the case of the latter group), and the testing accommodations, if any, that were given to them.

Although we argue for the importance of tracking the performance of different groups of students, it may not always be desirable to establish separate growth targets for each of these groups. The analyses reported by Kane and Staiger (2002) revealed that subgroup performance requirements increase the probability that measurement error in the test scores will prevent a school from meeting its accountability targets, and that diverse schools suffer from this problem the most. When subgroup requirements are included in accountability policies, as they are in NCLB, attention must be paid to the validity and reliability of the test-score information and the effects of the incentive system on students and schools.

Adopt Stable Statistical Indicators

Many states have experienced large fluctuations in school test scores from one year to the next that may threaten the credibility of their accountability systems in the eyes of educators and the public. For example, Maryland officials delayed the release of elementary and middle school scores in 2001 due to "wild swings" in scores (Libit, 2001). They were concerned that the changes were indicative of a mistake in their scoring and reporting system or that the changes were the result of school behaviors that the public would find unreasonable. As a result, they held up release of the scores while they investigated both possibilities.

Large annual increases or decreases in scores are generally acceptable if they can be traced back to identifiable causes and if these causes are clearly communicated to the public when the scores are released. They undermine the accountability system if they appear to occur for no reason. Such unreasonable changes cause the public to lose faith in the system and they may cause educators to worry about their own effectiveness. School staff members are likely to find it difficult to sustain any reform effort if they see their school's scores bounce around wildly from one year to the next. Unfortunately, there is a enough variability in school scores due to measurement error in the tests and changes in the population of students from one year to the next to cause large fluctuations in scores. Kane and Staiger (2002) calculated that 50 to 80 percent of the variation in school-gain scores was due to "non-persistent" factors such as sampling variation between cohorts of students. The problem of volatility is most severe for small schools. Therefore, there are certain to be large changes in some schools' scores that are unrelated to curriculum and instruction. This can have negative repercussions for the accountability system.

One way to reduce the volatility in annual scores is to base accountability decisions on two or more years of data rather than on a single year. Kentucky uses this approach, taking the average of two consecutive years as the indicator of growth. New two-year calculations are made each year to provide an annual indicator that is based on a more stable two-year average.

Another way to make changes in scores more stable is to base them on data from the same group of students, i.e., remove transient students and graduating students from the computation. This approach has shortcomings because it may exclude large numbers of students. However, these shortcomings may be offset by the advantages of having less volatile and more interpretable scores. To the extent that current knowledge permits, educators and policymakers should try to design accountability indicators that are maximally reflective of real differences and minimally reflective of measurement and sampling errors.

DESIGNING SYSTEMS THAT HAVE POSITIVE EFFECTS ON PRACTICE

This section describes ways to design accountability systems that are likely to lead to improvements in instruction while minimizing changes that inflate scores. We offer broad guidelines that should help states adopt systems that will promote their goals.

Conduct Ongoing Research and Evaluation of Effects on Practice

Earlier, we discussed the importance of an evaluative function in state testing programs. In addition to monitoring the technical quality of tests, states should evaluate the consequences of the system for school and classroom practice. Information about changes in teaching is relevant to the previous discussion of the validity of scores in tested and nontested subjects, and it is also important for its own sake. As we have noted previously, if teachers focus instruction on features of a test, such as specific question formats, then test scores may rise while student understanding of the underlying concepts remains unchanged. In addition, information about instruction and its relationship to student outcomes can help guide school reform efforts. It would be especially helpful to know what changes in instruction are made in response to different kinds of information and incentives. In particular, we need to know how teachers interpret information from tests and how they use it to modify instruction.

A variety of indicators may be designed to understand how schools and teachers respond, and to examine possible negative effects, such as inappropriate narrowing of the curriculum. These may include teacher or principal questionnaires, classroom observations, and the collection of artifacts such as lesson plans in both tested and nontested subjects. Because the methods that are most likely to provide valid information (e.g., classroom observations) are also likely to be expensive, a tiered data collection approach may be most effective. For example, observations could be conducted in a small, random sample of classrooms, with artifacts collected in a larger sample and questionnaires administered to an even larger group.

Align Teacher Professional Development and Curriculum with Standards and Assessments

Perhaps one of the best ways to promote desired responses on the part of teachers is to ensure that they understand and support the goals of the assessment program. Under pressure to raise scores, teachers are likely to make use of whatever information is available to them in their efforts to improve student achievement on the high-stakes test. Some of this information is likely to come from the test itself, and may lead to inappropriate focus on a particular set of items or item types. It is possible that this excessive emphasis on the test could be mitigated through efforts by the state to communicate the standards and goals of the test to teachers so that they have a clear sense of where they should be going. Publishing clear content standards is part of this, but states should do more than what most are currently doing to ensure that teachers understand and use the standards in their instruction.

Providing curriculum materials that support the goals of the assessment program is one important step states or districts can take. This is especially likely to be successful if teachers become convinced that they can raise scores by following the curriculum and that they do not need to focus on a particular test. Efforts to build tests that reflect important cognitive processes, as we discussed earlier, need to be accompanied by efforts to ensure that teachers understand these processes so that they can incorporate them into their instruction, and this includes providing materials and curricula that support these goals.

States or districts should also offer professional development that is carefully designed to promote the desired skills and knowledge, and it should be offered on an ongoing basis to both new and experienced teachers. This professional development could take a number of forms, including activities that directly support the accountability system. For example, in several states and districts, teachers participate in scoring open-ended assessment items, and in our experience, many teachers find that this activity is extremely beneficial professionally.

This advice is consistent with the idea of systemic reform, in which all components of the education system are aligned to promote common goals (Smith and O'Day, 1991), but we would argue even more strongly than most systemic reform advocates for the direct involvement of teachers in the process of developing, implementing, scoring, and using the results from high-stakes tests. It seems clear that aligning the components of the system and providing appropriate professional development should, at a minimum, increase teachers' political support for test-based accountability policies while also mitigating some of the concerns that teachers and their representatives have expressed. Although there is no empirical evidence to suggest that this strategy will reduce inappropriate responses to high-stakes testing, such as excessive test preparation, being better informed about the development and use of tests is likely to make teachers more responsive to these concerns. Additional research needs to be done to determine the importance of alignment for promoting positive effects of test-based accountability.

Clarify the Desired Balance Between Accountability Purposes and Instructional Purposes

One of the most problematic trade-offs arises from the desire for tests that function as effective tools of accountability while also providing instructional feedback to teachers. Given many teachers' perceptions that testing takes up large amounts of class time, it is natural that they would want those tests to provide data that could be used to improve instruction. However, it is important to keep in mind that requiring tests to serve multiple purposes sometimes results in a reduction in the utility of the test for any one of those purposes. The constraints of current large-scale testing systems make it difficult to design tests that have the features necessary to make them instructionally useful—e.g., prompt reporting of results or material tied closely to the curriculum of a given school or classroom—and that also meet the technical criteria necessary for high-stakes accountability purposes. It is important that states clarify the purpose of their testing programs as a basis for making decisions among competing demands and that they monitor the degree to which the tests are serving that purpose.

The guidelines published by the Commission on Instructionally Supportive Assessment (2001) represent a recent effort to promote the use of tests that serve both accountability and instructional purposes. The Commission notes that some of its recommendations, if implemented piecemeal, could threaten the validity of tests for large-scale accountability purposes. For example, states that follow its recommendations to limit accountability tests to a relatively small number of standards must also follow its later recommendation to enact a policy to keep teachers from narrowing the curriculum. To accomplish this, states may wish to provide teachers with optional classroom assessments that align with nontested content standards. If this is done, states should monitor teachers' use of the optional assessments and perhaps adopt an audit testing mechanism that would provide information on the effects of the system on content that is not part of the accountability tests.

Create Incentives That Promote Desired Goals

The one consistent theme in the existing research is that high-stakes tests elicit strong responses from schools and teachers, although there is disagreement about the nature of those responses and whether they are on balance beneficial or harmful. It is clear from the earlier discussions in this book that we currently do not know enough about test-based accountability to design a system that is immune from the problems we have discussed, and it is unlikely that such a system will ever exist. We do know, however, that the specific features of accountability systems influence responses, and it may be possible to develop a system with features designed to maximize desirable responses and minimize undesirable ones. States should consider the likely effects of their decisions about performance levels, annual progress targets, test formats, and other features of their testing programs on teacher and administrator behaviors.

As an example, consider the use of performance levels determined by cut scores. In a system that categorizes students as proficient or not proficient (i.e., whether their score is above or below a single cut score), teachers who want to maximize improvement on the accountability index should focus their instructional efforts on those students whose performance is slightly below the cut score. Because improvement in such a system is determined by the number of students who move from one side of the cut score to the other, focusing on those students is the most effective way to improve the school's standing.

By contrast, in a system that does not use cut scores but instead uses the overall average scores to make accountability decisions, upward movement of students at any point in the score scale will improve the school's standing. Some current systems are designed with these broad incentives in mind. California's Academic Performance Index (API), for example, categorizes students into five performance levels (or "bins") from the low end to the high end of the distribution so that movement throughout the score scale would affect the API. In addition, the system places greater weight on movement at the lower end of the score scale so that teachers and schools have a somewhat stronger incentive to focus on low-performing than on high-performing students. As this example illustrates, decisions about whether to use cut scores, how many to use, and where to place them affect the nature of the incentives in an accountability system and may directly affect the ways in which teachers and schools allocate their instructional resources.

Incentives are also influenced by the format of the test (e.g., inclusion of essay exams is likely to result in greater attention being paid to teaching writing), the frequency of administration, and the nature of the consequences attached to performance.

The way in which systems of rewards and sanctions are designed is especially important. For example, some states and districts that reward teachers have chosen to base decisions on performance at the school level, so that all teachers within a school receive the same reward. This policy is intended to motivate teachers to work together toward common goals and to prevent the dissension that may result when teachers feel they are competing with their colleagues. In addition, schools sometimes create their own incentives, such as pizza parties for students, that are not part of the formal accountability system.

States need to carefully consider the objectives they are trying to achieve—e.g., whether reducing gaps among high- and low-scoring students is important, or whether it is sufficient to achieve improvement for all students—and then design an accountability system with features that are likely to help them reach these objectives. They must also ensure that incentives for students and incentives for educators are coordinated so that teachers are not held accountable for scores on tests on which students may not be motivated to perform, and so that students are not held accountable for learning material that teachers may not present to them. At the same time, states must recognize that they cannot completely control the incentive system or how students, teachers, and administrators will respond to it.

Consider Each Policy's Potential Effects on Equity

One of the driving forces behind current testing reforms is a desire to improve the performance and opportunities of students who have traditionally experienced low levels of academic success. Accountability systems have been applauded for reducing performance gaps among racial/ethnic groups and for setting high standards for all students. As we have discussed, however, simple inspection of scores on the accountability test may provide misleading information about actual improvement. Furthermore, it may mask differences in students' exposure to curriculum or opportunities to learn. As states monitor their accountability efforts, and as they consider adopting a new policy or practice, they should pay particular attention to issues of equity.

We are unable to offer clear-cut guidance on how to ensure equity, however. Questions remain about the actual effects on low-scoring students and about possible negative consequences of test-based accountability policies on the resources and opportunities provided to students from impoverished backgrounds. There are concerns about school-level accountability—e.g., whether schools in poor neighborhoods will be disproportionately excluded from rewards or affected by sanctions. Other questions concern individual students—whether high school exit exams will result in greater dropout and retention rates among some groups of students, or whether English-language learners and students with disabilities will be harmed by an emphasis on standardized test scores.

There is some limited evidence that educators' responses to test-based accountability vary according to the characteristics of their student populations, with teachers of poor and minority students most likely to engage in excessive test preparation (McNeil and Valenzuela, 2000). And, as we discussed earlier, the practice of requiring separate groups to meet targets may actually result in reduced chances for rewards at ethnically diverse schools (Kane and Staiger, 2002). These and other studies suggest there is a need for attention to equity considerations, but the larger questions of whether test-based accountability enhances equity, and what specific policies do this most effectively, remain unanswered. Equity should be a major focus of future research efforts.

POLITICAL CONSIDERATIONS

This section is brief because there is very limited evidence to guide thinking about political issues. However, the viability of the ambitious accountability plans that have been put forth requires support from a variety of stakeholders, so consideration of the political environment is crucial.

Facilitate Integration of Political and Professional Perspectives

In Chapter Five, we discussed some of the political aspects of test-based accountability. One primary source of tension surrounding these systems arises from the fact that members of different stakeholder groups often have very different goals for what accountability systems should accomplish. Furthermore, they sometimes use different language to describe their concerns, making effective communication difficult. All stakeholders in public education, including policymakers, technical experts, and parents, should be sensitive to these different points of view, but the burden of understanding falls most directly on those charged with making and implementing policy. Policymakers need to go out of their way to make their messages clear and to understand the information that they are being provided. At the same time, members of the technical measurement community must move beyond the role of critic and provide suggestions for alternatives to current accountability approaches.

To facilitate these objectives, states could staff their assessment offices with people who are adept at interacting with members of these various groups (e.g., technical experts who understand the concerns of policymakers and parents), and involve them in communication outreach efforts. These same concerns relate to the score reports that are generated by the testing program. States must be extremely careful in how they communicate test results to the public so that expectations are realistic and appropriate. Perhaps above all, stakeholders need to understand the limitations of current tests as indicators of school or student success, and must understand their own roles in ensuring that schools, teachers, and students have the necessary resources to improve their performance.

Incorporate Parents' Perspectives

A stakeholder group that has been largely ignored in research to date is families, particularly the parents and guardians who are responsible for making decisions about their children's education. Although teachers are often considered the primary targets of accountability policies, parents are perhaps an equally critical stakeholder group because of the profound effects their actions (e.g., how much they read to their children or what steps they take to help their children to overcome academic difficulties) have on student learning.

To ensure that test-based accountability is serving the needs of parents, policymakers need to be attentive to the parents' needs and concerns. For example, do parents want information about test score levels, test score gains, or both? Are they interested in a broader range of measures than is currently included in school reports? What do they believe test score gains tell them about what and how much their children are learning? A better understanding of how parents interpret test-score information and what kind of information would be most informative to them would help educators and policymakers design more-effective systems and increase public support for those systems.

It is also important to understand the role of parents in student testing and the decisions parents make as a result of test-score information. How do they help their students prepare? To what extent do they make use of various test-preparation resources? How do they use test-score data to make decisions about where to send their children to school, particularly in choice-based systems? And to what extent does the publication of test-score data or the provision of rewards and sanctions affect parents' efforts to influence education policies and practices and their children's schools? Parental support is critical for ensuring that test-based accountability accomplishes its objectives, and efforts need to be made to ensure that the parent perspective is part of the deliberative process.

Explore Costs and Benefits of Alternative Approaches

Policymakers need to be attentive to the costs (both expenditures and opportunity costs) that accountability systems impose on states, schools, and students. The cost issue consists of three related elements: (1) assessing the true costs of various testing alternatives, (2) comparing costs and benefits, and (3) designing new alternatives that reflect realistic cost-benefit compromises. All three of these elements involve subjective judgments and thus have political dimensions.

Almost all of the advice we have offered to this point for improving accountability systems will result in added costs to the state and to local schools (in the form of time being taken away from other activities). To date, few states have been willing to absorb what they perceive to be the additional costs of such improvements. Yet, this point of view may be shortsighted. First, we do not have an accurate assessment of the additional costs. In most states, any proposal for new expenditures faces an uphill battle. However, many of these recommended reforms are relatively inexpensive in comparison with the total cost of education. This equation is seldom examined. Second, few people have given adequate attention to the long-term benefits of better accountability systems. If student achievement improves and negative consequences are avoided, the net result may be a lowering of total educational costs over time.

Part of the reason these issues are rarely considered may be that no one has produced a good estimate of the cost of an improved accountability system in comparison with its benefits. There have been some attempts to estimate the costs of various types of testing. For example, Stecher and Klein (1997) estimated the cost of conducting hands-on science performance assessments that produced reliable individual scores at $60 to $80 per student. This may represent a reasonable upper limit for subject-matter testing because science performance assessments are among the most complex tests to develop, administer, and score. Hoxby's (2002) analysis suggests that the costs of accountability systems that use more-traditional forms of testing are lower than most critics believe, even when they incorporate quality assurance procedures such as proctors and frequent changes in test form.

Nevertheless, our knowledge of the costs of alternative accountability systems is still somewhat limited. Policymakers need to know how much it would cost to change their current systems to be responsive to criticisms such as those described in this book. These estimates need to consider all of the associated costs, including possible opportunity costs associated with increased testing time and increased test preparation time.

Furthermore, if high-stakes outcomes for students continue to increase, we need to understand the costs imposed on families by these systems; e.g., how much money is spent on test preparation materials by parents who are worried about whether their children will graduate or be promoted? Ongoing estimates of these various costs should be incorporated into states' evaluation systems.

Over time, by aggregating cost information for different kinds of systems, we may acquire a better sense of the true costs imposed by test-based accountability. This is a necessary condition for making the difficult cost-benefit comparisons described above. It is also important to take a long-term view when thinking about expanding accountability systems. A long-term agenda that includes periodic audit testing, item refreshment, assessments of other subjects, and other checks on the system might go a long way toward optimizing the system while keeping costs at a reasonable level.

CONCLUSION

The primary goal of most education reforms is the improvement of student learning. The current popularity of test-based accountability systems stems from the widespread belief that setting clear goals and providing incentives will lead to improved achievement. Existing research has been very helpful in identifying limitations in current test-based accountability systems that can inform future accountability efforts.

This chapter offered research-based advice for policymakers and practitioners who are charged with designing or improving accountability systems. Above all, the discussions in this chapter indicate that the details of how an accountability system is implemented do in fact matter. Much of the policy debate has assumed that accountability is either an effective or a dangerous approach for reforming education, but as with all reforms, the truth is not that simple. The specific features of an accountability system are likely to have a tremendous effect on the degree to which that system promotes desirable outcomes.

However, there is still much about these systems that is not well understood. Lack of research-based knowledge about the quality of scores and the mechanisms through which high-stakes testing programs operate limits our ability to improve these systems. As a result, our discussions also identified unanswered questions that should be raised when legislators enact new accountability requirements, when state departments of education contract with test developers or design new testing systems, and when the public is asked for input on educational testing policy.

It may not be possible for states to undertake the research that is needed to answer all these questions on their own, but they can play an important role in the research process. Past research on accountability has had to overcome a number of obstacles, including lack of access to good data, lack of access to the tests themselves, and an unwillingness among many politicians and policymakers to support further research on an approach that they have already decided is effective. However, if efforts are not made to understand ways to improve test-based accountability, it is likely that many of the negative effects we have discussed will become more pronounced and will reduce public support for accountability policies.

With the help and encouragement of state policymakers, future research can elucidate the mechanisms though which test-based accountability ultimately affects student learning. Future research can also identify ways in which the benefits of these systems can be maximized while the negative consequences are minimized, if not eliminated altogether.

Educators, policymakers, and researchers should take a two-pronged approach to improving the quality of test-based accountability systems: Incremental improvements to existing systems, based on current research on testing and accountability, should be combined with long-term research and development efforts that may ultimately lead to a major redesign of these systems. Success in this endeavor will require the thoughtful engagement of educators, policymakers, and researchers in discussions and debates about tests and testing policies.

A number of academic and research institutions conduct work on test-based accountability and a number of other organizations have published information on the subject. It is impossible to list every resource here, but the following are some good places to start on the Web for information on the subject.

RESEARCH ON ASSESSMENT AND ACCOUNTABILITY

The National Center for Research on Evaluation, Standards, and Student Testing (CRESST) is a partnership that includes the University of California, Los Angeles; the University of Colorado; Stanford University; RAND; the University of Pittsburgh; the University of Southern California; the Educational Testing Service; and the University of Cambridge, United Kingdom. CRESST conducts and disseminates research that focuses on the assessment of educational quality and provides assessment resources to parents, policymakers, and others. The CRESST Web site is at: **http://www.cse.ucla.edu**

- The CRESST site also provides a glossary of commonly used measurement terms, which can be found at: **http://www.cse.ucla.edu/CRESST/pages/glossary.htm**

- CRESST, in collaboration with the Consortium for Policy Research in Education and the Education Commission of the States, recently published the Standards for Educational Accountability Systems. The standards can be found at: **http://www.cse.ucla.edu/CRESST/Newsletters/polbrf54.pdf**

The Consortium for Policy Research in Education (CPRE) conducts research to improve education policy and practice. It includes five partner institutions: the University of Pennsylvania, Harvard University, Stanford University, the University of Michigan, and the University of Wisconsin–Madison. The CPRE Web site can be found at: **http://www.cpre.org**

- Included in CPRE's work on accountability is a summary of each of the states' policies, "Assessment and Accountability Systems, 50 State Profiles," which can be found at: **http://www.cpre.org/ Publications/Publications_Accountability.htm**

The American Educational Research Association (AERA) is a professional organization for researchers who study education. Its primary goal is to advance education research and the practical application of that research. The organization publishes several professional journals as well as books, policy statements, and other products. The AERA Web site is at: **http://aera.net/**

- AERA's Position statement on high-stakes testing in pre-K–12 education is available at: **http://aera.net/about/policy/stakes. htm**

- AERA, in conjunction with the National Council on Measurement in Education and the American Psychological Association, publishes the *Standards for Educational and Psychological Testing*, which is available for purchase at: **http://aera.net/ products/standards.htm**

SUMMARIES OF STATE ASSESSMENT AND ACCOUNTABILITY SYSTEMS

Several organizations have summarized features of state systems, and some have published evaluative information on the quality of standards and assessments. One of these sites, CPRE, is listed above. The following Web sites provide the results of some other efforts:

American Federation of Teachers (AFT), AFL-CIO, *Making Standards Matter* is at: **http://www.aft.org/**

Council of Chief State School Officers (CCSSO), *State Education Accountability Reports and Indicator Reports: Status of Reports Across the States—2000* can be found at: **http://www.ccsso.org/pdfs/ AccountabilityReport2000.pdf**

Education Commission of the States is at: **http://www.ecs.org**

- This site includes the report *No State Left Behind: The Challenges and Opportunities of ESEA 2001* at: **http://www.ecs.org/ecsmain. asp?page=/html/special/ESEA_main.htm**

Education Week *Quality Counts* report (search for "Quality Counts") is at: **http://www.edweek.org**

Thomas B. Fordham Foundation *Standards Testing and Accountability* is at: **http://www.edexcellence.net/topics/standards.html**

OTHER RESOURCES

The U.S. Department of Education's Web site provides information on and links to publications, programs, legislation, and other initiatives, such as the following two program sites. The department's Web site is at: **http://www.ed.gov/index.jsp**

- Information on the No Child Left Behind legislation can be found at: **http://www.nochildleftbehind.gov/**

- *The Nation's Report Card* from the National Center for Education Statistics, National Assessment of Educational Progress, can be found at: **http://nces.ed.gov/nationsreportcard/**

The National Center for the Improvement of Educational Assessment (also called the Center for Assessment) supports states and districts in their efforts to design and implement accountability systems. The organization provides a number of services including technical assistance and monitoring, and its Web site includes publications that can be downloaded. The center's Web site is at: **http://www.nciea. org/index.html**

Achieve, Inc., founded by governors and business leaders following a 1996 National Education Summit, is an independent organization that works with states to improve standards, assessments, and accountability policies. Its ongoing projects include a benchmarking initiative designed to help states compare their standards and assessments with those of other states and countries. The Achieve, Inc., Web site is at: **http://www.achieve.org/**

National Education Association (NEA), the nation's oldest professional organization for teachers, has produced a guide that explains testing and accountability to parents. The NEA guide is available at: **http://www.nea.org/parents/testingguide/**

Achieve, Inc. (1999). National Education Summit Briefing Book. Washington, D.C.

Achieve, Inc. (2000). Setting the Record Straight. Achieve Policy Brief, Issue Number One. Washington, D.C.

Achieve, Inc. (2002). Aiming Higher: The Next Decade of Education Reform in Maryland. Washington, D.C.

Airasian, P. W. (1987). State mandated testing and educational reform: Context and consequences. American Journal of Education, 95, 393–412.

Airasian, P. W., and G. F. Madaus. (1983). Linking testing and instruction: Policy issues. Journal of Educational Measurement, 20 (2), 103–118.

American Educational Research Association. (2000). Position statement of the American Educational Research Association concerning high-stakes testing in pre K–12 education. Educational Researcher, 29(8), 24–25.

American Educational Research Association, American Psychological Association, and National Council on Measurement in Education. (1999). Standards for Educational and Psychological Testing. Washington, D.C.

American Federation of Teachers. (2001). Making Standards Matter 2001. Washington, D.C.

Anderson, N. E., F. F. Jenkins, and K. E. Miller. (1996). NAEP Inclusion Criteria and Testing Accommodations. Findings from the NAEP 1995 Field Test in Mathematics. Washington, D.C.: Educational Testing Service.

Astin, A., L. Tsui, and J. Avalos. (1996). Degree Attainment at American Colleges and Universities: Effect of Race, Gender, and Institutional Type. Washington, D.C: American Council on Education.

Baker, E. L., R. L. Linn, J. L. Herman, and D. Koretz. (2002). Standards for Educational Accountability Systems (CRESST Policy Brief 5). Los Angeles: National Center for Research on Evaluation, Standards, and Student Testing.

Baron, J., and M. F. Norman. (1992). SATs, achievement tests, and high-school class rank as predictors of college performance. Educational and Psychological Measurement, 52, 1047–1055.

Baxter, G. P., R. J. Shavelson, S. R. Goldman, and J. Pine. (1992). Evaluation of procedure-based scoring for hands-on science assessment. Journal of Educational Measurement, 29(1), 1–17.

Bennett, R. E. (1998). Reinventing Assessment. Princeton, N.J.: Educational Testing Service.

Bishop, J. H. (1986). The impact of curriculum based external examination systems on learning and schooling. International Journal of Educational Research, 23(8).

Bishop, J. H., and F. Mane. (Winter 1999). The New York state reform strategy: The incentive effects of minimum competency exams. CEIC Review. Philadelphia: The National Center on Education in Inner Cities.

Bolger, N., and T. Kellaghan. (1990). Method of measurement and gender differences in scholastic achievement. Journal of Educational Measurement, 27, 165–174.

Borko, H., and R. Elliott. (1999). Hands-on pedagogy versus hands-off accountability. Phi Delta Kappan, 80(5), 394–400.

Borko, H., R. Elliott, and K. Uchiyama. (1999). Professional development: A key to Kentucky's educational reform effort. Paper presented at the annual meeting of the American Educational Research Association. Montreal.

Bowman, D. H. (September 5, 2001). Delayed again: Arizona moves high school exit exam to 2006. Education Week.

Breland, H. M., D. O. Danow, H. D. Kahn, M. Y. Kubota, and M. W. Bonner. (1994). Performance versus objective testing and gender: An exploratory study of an Advanced Placement history examination. Journal of Educational Measurement, 31, 275–293.

Brownstein, R. (July 24, 2001a). Belatedly, a front is forming to fight education legislation. Los Angeles Times, A14.

Brownstein, R. (August 2, 2001b). Bush eases his position on school accountability issue. Los Angeles Times, A14.

Business Roundtable. (2001a). Assessing and Addressing the "Testing Backlash." Washington, D.C.

Business Roundtable. (2001b). Making Standards Work: Public Attitudes About Standards and Testing. Washington, D.C.

California Department of Education. (1998). Steering by Results: A High-Stakes Rewards and Interventions Program for California Schools and Students. Sacramento.

Campbell, D. T., and D. W. Fiske. (1959). Convergent and discriminant validation by the multitrait-multimethod matrix. Psychological Bulletin, 56, 81–105.

Carlson, D. (2000). All students or the ones we taught? Presentation at the Council of Chief State School Officers Annual National Conference on Large-Scale Assessment. Snowbird, Utah.

Carnoy, M. (2001). Do School Vouchers Improve Student Performance? Washington, D.C.: Economic Policy Institute.

Carnoy, M., S. Loeb, and T. L. Smith. (2000). Do higher state test scores in Texas make for better high school outcomes? Paper presented at the annual meeting of the American Educational Research Association. New Orleans.

Cizek, G. J. (1998). Filling in the blanks: Putting standardized tests to the test. Fordham Report, 2(11). http://www.edexcellence.net/library/cizek.pdf (last accessed May 15, 2002).

Cole, N. S., and M. J. Zieky. (2001). The new faces of fairness. Journal of Educational Measurement, 38(4), 369–382.

Commission on Instructionally Supportive Assessment. (2001). Building Tests to Support Instruction and Accountability. Report prepared for the American Association of School Administrators, National Association of Elementary School Principals, National Association of Secondary School Principals, National Education Association, and National Middle School Association. Washington, D.C.

Consortium for Policy Research in Education. (2000). Assessment and Accountability Systems: 50 State Profiles. http://www.cpre.org/Publications/Publications_Accountability.htm (last accessed May 13, 2002).

Corbett, H. D., and B. L. Wilson. (1988). Raising the stakes in statewide mandatory minimum competency testing. In W. L. Boyd and C. T. Kerchner (eds.). The Politics of Excellence and Choice in Education: The 1987 Politics of Education Association Yearbook, 27–39. New York: Falmer Press.

Corbett, H. D., and B. L. Wilson. (1991). Testing, Reform, and Rebellion. Norwood, N.J.: Ablex Publishing.

Crocker, L., and J. Algina. (1986). Introduction to Classical and Modern Test Theory. Fort Worth, Tex.: Harcourt Brace Jovanovich.

Cronbach, L. J. (1971). Test validation. In R. L. Thorndike (ed.). Educational Measurement, 2nd ed., 443–507. Washington, D.C.: American Council on Education.

Cronbach, L. J. (1988). Five perspectives on validity argument. In H. Wainer and H. I. Braun (eds.). Test Validity, 3–17. Hillsdale, N.J.: Erlbaum.

Dallas Morning News. (November 13, 2000). TAAS gainers show more exemptions: Many improving schools omit special-ed students.

Darling-Hammond, L., and A. E. Wise. (1985). Beyond standardization: State standards and school improvement. The Elementary School Journal, 85, 315–336.

De Neufville, J. I., and S. E. Barton. (1987). Myths and the definition of policy problems. Policy Sciences, 20, 181–206.

Debra P. v. Turlington, 474 F. Supp. 244 (M.D. Fla 1979); aff'd in part, rev'd in part, 644 F.2d 397 (5th Cir., 1981).

Downs, A. (1957). An Economic Theory of Democracy. New York: Harper and Row.

Dunbar, S. B., D. Koretz, and H. D. Hoover. (1991). Quality control in the development and use of performance assessments. Applied Measurement in Education, 4(4), 289–304.

Education Commission of the States. (July 2001). High Stakes Assessment: State Modifications. Denver: ECS Clearinghouse. http://www.ecs.org/clearinghouse/28/12/2812.htm (last accessed May 10, 2002).

Education Week. (November 1, 2001). Quality Counts 2001. Bethesda, Md.

Elam, S. M., and L. C. Rose. (1995). The 27th annual Phi Delta Kappa/Gallup poll of the public's attitudes toward the public schools. Phi Delta Kappan, 77(1), 41–56.

Elam, S. M., L. C. Rose, and A. M. Gallup. (1996). The 28th annual Phi Delta Kappa/Gallup poll of the public's attitudes toward the public schools. Phi Delta Kappan, 78(1), 41–59.

Farhi, P. (November 17, 1996). Television's "sweeps" stakes: Season of the sensational called a contest out of control. The Washington Post, A1, A12.

Feldt, L. S., and R. L. Brennan. (1989). Reliability. In R. L. Linn (ed.), Educational Measurement, 3rd ed., 105–146. New York: Macmillan.

Feuer, M. (1992). Testing in American Schools: Asking the Right Questions. Report prepared for the U.S. Congress, Office of

Technology Assessment. OTA-SET-519. Washington, D.C.: U.S. Government Printing Office.

Firestone, W. A., D. Mayrowetz, and J. Fairman. (1998). Performance-based assessment and instructional change: The effects of testing in Maine and Maryland. Educational Evaluation and Policy Analysis, 20(2), 95–113.

Florida Department of Education. (2001). School Accountability Report Guidesheet. http://www.firn.edu/doe/schoolgrades/guide01. htm (last accessed June 11, 2002).

Fuller, B., G. Hayward, and M. Kirst. (1998). Californians Speak on Education and Reform Options. Berkeley, Calif.: Policy Analysis for California Education.

Gearhart, M., and J. L. Herman. (1998). Portfolio assessment: Whose work is it? Issues in the use of classroom assignments for accountability. Educational Assessment, 5(1), 41–55.

Gehring, J. (November 22, 2000). Mass. teachers blast state tests in new TV ads. Education Week, 1, 22.

General Accounting Office. (January 1993). Student Testing: Current Extent and Expenditures, with Cost Estimates for a National Examination. GAO/PEMD-93-8. Washington, D.C.

GI Forum et al. v. Texas Education Agency, et al. 87 F. Supp. 2d 667 (W.D. Tex. 2000).

Ginsburg, A. L., J. Noell, and V. W. Plisko. (1988). Lessons from the Wall Chart. Educational Evaluation and Policy Analysis, 10(1), 1–12.

Glaser, R. (2001). Conflicts, engagements, skirmishes, and attempts at peace. Educational Assessment, 7, 13–20.

Goertz, M. E., and M. C. Duffy. (2001). Assessment and Accountability Systems in the 50 States: 1999–2000. Philadelphia: Consortium for Policy Research in Education.

Goldhaber, D., and J. Hannaway. (2001). Accountability with a kicker: Observations on the Florida A+ Accountability Plan. Paper presented at the annual meeting of the Association of Public Policy and Management, Washington, D.C.

Goodnough, A. (December 8, 1999). Answers allegedly supplied in effort to raise test scores. New York Times.

Goslin, D. A. (1963). Teachers and Testing. New York: Russell Sage.

Goslin, D. A., R. R. Epstein, and B. A. Hallock. (1965). The Use of Standardized Tests in Elementary Schools. New York: Russell Sage.

Green, B. F. (1993). The Structural Validity and Generalizability of the 1992 Maryland State Assessment Program. Maryland State Department of Education. Baltimore.

Greenberger, S. S. (October 24, 2000). Critics intensify MCAS battle: Ballot questions, association vote are focus of effort. Boston Globe, B1.

Gruber, J. E. (1987). Controlling Bureaucracies: Dilemmas in Democratic Governance. Berkeley: University of California Press.

Hambleton, R. K. (1998). Setting performance standards on achievement tests. In L. N. Hansche (ed.). Handbook for the Development of Performance Standards: Meeting the Requirements of Title I, Chapter 10. Washington, D.C.: Council of Chief State School Officers and U.S. Department of Education.

Hambleton, R. K., J. Impara, W. Mehrens, and B. S. Plake. (2000). Psychometric Review of the Maryland School Performance Assessment Program (MSPAP). Maryland State Department of Education. Baltimore. http://www.abell.org/ (search "Publications" link; last accessed May 13, 2002).

Hambleton, R. K., R. M. Jaeger, D. Koretz, R. L. Linn, J. Millman, and S. E. Phillips. (1995). Review of the Measurement Quality of the Kentucky Instructional Results Information Systems, 1991–1994. A report prepared for the Office of Education Accountability, Kentucky General Assembly. Frankfort, Ky.: Office of Education Accountability.

Hambleton, R. K., R. M. Jaeger, B. S. Plake, and C. M. Mills. (1998). Handbook on Setting Standards on Performance Assessments. Washington, D.C.: Council of Chief State School Officers.

Hambleton, R. K., H. Swaminathan, and H. J. Rogers. (1991). Fundamentals of Item Response Theory. Newbury Park, Calif.: Sage.

Hamilton, L. S. (1998). Gender differences on high school science achievement tests: Do format and content matter? Educational Evaluation and Policy Analysis, 20, 179–195.

Hamilton, L. S., S. P. Klein, and W. Lorie. (2000). Using Web-Based Testing for Large-Scale Assessments. IP-196. Santa Monica, Calif.: RAND.

Hamilton, L. S., E. M. Nussbaum, H. Kupermintz, J.I.M. Kerkhoven, and R. E. Snow. (1995). Enhancing the validity and usefulness of large scale educational assessments: II. NELS: 88 science achievement. American Educational Research Journal, 32, 555–581.

Hamilton, L. S., E. M. Nussbaum, and R. E. Snow. (1997). Interview procedures for validating science assessments. Applied Measurement in Education, 10(2), 181–200.

Haney, W. (1981). Validity, vaudeville, and values: A short history of social concerns over standardized testing. American Psychologist, 36(10), 1021–1034.

Haney, W. (2000). The myth of the Texas miracle in education. Educational Policy Analysis Archives, 8(41). http://epaa.asu.edu/epaa/v8n41/ (last accessed May 10, 2002).

Hansche, L. N. (1998). Handbook for the Development of Performance Standards: Meeting the Requirements of Title I. Washington, D.C.: Council of Chief State School Officers and U.S. Department of Education.

Harris, A. M., and S. T. Carlton. (1993). Patterns of gender differences in mathematics items on the Scholastic Aptitude Test. Applied Measurement in Education, 6, 137–151.

Hauser, R. M., D. I. Pager, and S. J. Simmons. (August 2000). Race-ethnicity, social background, and grade retention. Presented at the annual meeting of the American Sociological Association, Washington, D.C.

Hedges, L. V., and A. Nowell. (1998). Black-white test score convergence since 1965. In C. Jencks and M. Phillips (eds.). The Black-White Test Score Gap, 149–181. Washington, D.C.: Brookings Institution Press.

Herman, J. L., and S. Golan. (n.d.). Effects of Standardized Testing on Teachers and Learning—Another Look. CSE Technical Report 334. Los Angeles: National Center for Research on Evaluation, Standards, and Student Testing.

Heubert, J. P., and R. M. Hauser (eds.). (1999). High Stakes: Testing for Tracking, Promotion, and Graduation. Washington, D.C.: National Academy Press.

Hieronymus, A. N., and H. D. Hoover. (1986). Manual for School Administrators, Levels 5–14, ITBS Forms G/H. Chicago: The Riverside Publishing Company.

Hochschild, J., and B. Scott. (1998). Trends: Governance and reform of public education in the United States. Public Opinion Quarterly, 62(1), 79–120.

Hoover, D. D., A. N. Hieronymous, D. A. Frisbie, S. B. Dunbar, K. R. Oberley, N. K. Cantor, G. B. Bray, J. C. Lewis, and A. L. Qualls-Payne. (1994). Iowa Tests of Basic Skills Interpretive Guide for School Administrators, Levels 5–14. Chicago: The Riverside Publishing Company.

Hoxby, C. M. (2002). The cost of accountability. In W. M. Evers and H. J. Walberg (eds.). School Accountability, 47–74. Stanford, Calif.: Hoover Institution Press.

Immerwahr, J. (1997). What Our Children Need: South Carolinians Look at Public Education. New York: Public Agenda.

Jaeger, R. M. (1982). The final hurdle: Minimum competency achievement testing. In G. R. Austin and H. Garber (eds.). The Rise and Fall of National Test Scores. New York: Academic Press.

Johnson, J., and J. Immerwahr. (1994). First Things First: What Americans Expect from the Public Schools. New York: Public Agenda.

Jones, G., B. D. Jones, B. Hardin, L. Chapman, T. Yarbrough, and M. Davis. (1999). The impact of high-stakes testing on teachers and students in North Carolina. Phi Delta Kappan, 81(3), 199–203.

Kane, T. J., and D. O. Staiger. (2001). Improving School Accountability Measures. http://papers.nber.org/papers/W8156 (last accessed May 10, 2002).

Kane, T. J., and D. O. Staiger. (2002). Volatility in school test scores: Implications for test-based accountability systems. In D. Ravitch (ed.). Brookings Papers on Education Policy 2002, 235–283. Washington, D.C.: Brookings Institution Press.

Kane, T. J., D. O. Staiger, and J. Geppert. (2001). Assessing the definition of "Adequate Yearly Progress" in the House and Senate education bills. Working paper. http://www.brookings.edu/dybdocroot/gs/brown/housesenate6.pdf (last accessed May 13, 2002).

Kingdon, J. W. (1993). Politicians, self-interest, and ideas. In G. E. Marcus and R. L. Hanson (eds.). Reconsidering the Democratic Public, 73–89. College Station, Pa.: Pennsylvania State University Press.

Klein, S. P., L. S. Hamilton, D. F. McCaffrey, and B. M. Stecher. (2000). What Do Test Scores in Texas Tell Us? IP-202. Santa Monica, Calif.: RAND.

Klein, S. P., J. Jovanovic, B. M. Stecher, D. McCaffrey, R. J. Shavelson, E. Haertel, G. Solano-Flores, and K. Comfort. (1997). Gender and racial/ethnic differences on performance assessments in science. Educational Evaluation and Policy Analysis, 19, 83–97.

Klein, S. P., and M. Orlando. (2000). CUNY's Testing Program: Characteristics, Results, and Implications for Policy and Research. MR-1249-CAE. Santa Monica, Calif.: RAND.

Koretz, D. (1986). Trends in Educational Achievement. Washington, D.C.: Congressional Budget Office, U.S. Congress.

Koretz, D. (1992). State and national assessment. In M. C. Alkin (ed.). Encyclopedia of Educational Research, 6th ed., 1262–1267. Washington, D.C.: American Educational Research Association.

Koretz, D. (1997). The Assessment of Students with Disabilities in Kentucky. CSE Technical Report 431. Los Angeles: National Center for Research on Evaluation, Standards, and Student Testing.

Koretz, D., and S. I. Barron. (1998). The Validity of Gains on the Kentucky Instructional Results Information System (KIRIS). MR-1014-EDU. Santa Monica, Calif.: RAND.

Koretz, D., S. Barron, K. Mitchell, and B. Stecher. (1996a). The Perceived Effects of the Kentucky Instructional Results Information System (KIRIS). MR-792-PCT/FF. Santa Monica, Calif.: RAND.

Koretz, D., and L. S. Hamilton. (2000). Assessment of students with disabilities in Kentucky: Inclusion, student performance, and validity. Educational Evaluation and Policy Analysis, 22, 255–272.

Koretz, D., R. L. Linn, S. B. Dunbar, and L. A Shepard. (1991). The effects of high-stakes testing on achievement: Preliminary findings about generalization across tests. Paper presented at the annual meeting of the American Educational Research Association, Chicago.

Koretz, D., D. McCaffrey, and L. Hamilton. (2001). Toward a Framework for Validating Gains Under High-Stakes Conditions. CSE Technical Report 551. Los Angeles: National Center for Research on Evaluation, Standards, and Student Testing.

Koretz, D., K. Mitchell, S. Barron, and S. Keith. (1996b). The Perceived Effects of the Maryland School Performance Assessment Program. CSE Technical Report 409. Los Angeles: National Center for Research on Evaluation, Standards, and Student Testing.

Koretz, D., B. Stecher, S. Klein, and D. McCaffrey. (1994). The Vermont portfolio assessment program: Findings and implications. Educational Measurement: Issues and Practice, 13(3), 5–16.

Kupermintz, H., M. M. Ennis, L. S. Hamilton, J. E. Talbert, and R. E. Snow. (1995). Enhancing the validity and usefulness of large scale educational assessments: I. NELS: 88 mathematics achievement. American Educational Research Journal, 32, 525–554.

Lane, S., and C. Stone. (April 2001). Consequences of assessment and accountability programs. Paper presented at the annual meeting of the American Educational Research Association, Seattle.

Lemann, N. (July 2, 2001). Testing limits. The New Yorker, 28–34.

Lepper, M. R., and J. Henderlong. (2000). Turning "play" into "work" and "work" into "play": 25 years of research on intrinsic versus extrinsic motivation. In C. Sansone and J. M. Harackiewicz (eds.). Intrinsic and Extrinsic Motivation: The Search for Optimal Motivation and Performance, 257–307. San Diego: Academic Press.

Libit, H. (November 7, 2001). State delays release of MSPAP test results: Officials will review "wild swings" in scores. The Baltimore Sun.

Linn, R. L. (1982). Ability testing: Individual differences, prediction, and differential prediction. In A. K. Wigdor and W. R. Garner (eds.). Ability Testing: Uses, Consequences, and Controversies, 335–388. Washington, D.C.: National Academy Press.

Linn, R. L. (1993). Educational assessment: Expanded expectations and challenges. Educational Evaluation and Policy Analysis, 15(1), 1–16.

Linn, R. L. (2000). Assessments and accountability. Educational Researcher, 29(2): 4–16.

Linn, R. L. (2001). The Design and Evaluation of Educational Assessment and Accountability Systems. CSE Technical Report 539. Los Angeles: National Center for Research on Evaluation, Standards, and Student Testing.

Lord, F. N., and M. R. Novick. (1968). Statistical Theories of Mental Test Scores. Reading, Mass.: Addison-Wesley.

Madaus, G. F. (1983). The Courts, Validity, and Minimum Competency Testing. Hingham, Mass.: Kluwer-Nijhoff Publishing.

Madaus, G. F. (1988). The influence of testing on the curriculum. In L. N. Tanner (ed.). Critical Issues in Curriculum: Eighty-Seventh Yearbook of the National Society for the Study of Education, 83–121. Chicago: University of Chicago Press. Also in L. N. Tanner (ed.). The Politics of Reforming School Administration. London, England: Falmer Press.

Manzo, K. K. (May 16, 2001). Protests over state testing widespread. Education Week, 1, 26.

Mass Insight. (1997). Education Reform: The Public's View of Standards and Tests. Cambridge, Mass.

Massachusetts Department of Education. (October 1999). Massachusetts Comprehensive Assessment System. 1998 Technical Report. Malden, Mass.

Mazzeo, J., A. P. Schmitt, and C. A. Bleistein. (1993). Sex-Related Performance Differences on Constructed-Response and Multiple-Choice Sections of Advanced Placement Examinations. CB Report No. 92-7; ETS RR-93-5. New York: College Entrance Examination Board.

McDonnell, L. M. (1994a). Assessment policy as persuasion and regulation. American Journal of Education, 102(4), 394–420.

McDonnell, L. M. (1994b). Policymakers' Views of Student Assessment. MR-348. Santa Monica, Calif.: RAND.

McDonnell, L. M., M. J. McLaughlin, and P. Morison (eds.). (1997). Educating One and All: Students with Disabilities and Standards-Based Reform. Washington, D.C.: National Academy Press.

McFarlane, C. (May 2, 2001). Teachers and state in MCAS ad war; union says public support is dropping. Worcester Telegram and Gazette, A1.

McLaughlin, M. W. (1987). Learning from experience: Lessons from policy implementation. Educational Evaluation and Policy Analysis, 9(2), 171–178.

McNeil, L. M. (2000). Creating new inequalities: Contradictions of reform. Phi Delta Kappan, 81, 729–734.

McNeil, L. M., and A. Valenzuela. (2000). The Harmful Impact of the TAAS System of Testing in Texas: Beneath the Accountability Rhetoric. Cambridge, Mass.: Harvard University Civil Rights Project.

Mehrens, W. A. (July 14, 1998). Consequences of assessment: What is the evidence? Education Policy Analysis Archives, 6(13). http://epaa.asu.edu/epaa/v6n13.html (last accessed May 13, 2002).

Mehrens, W. A. (1999). The CBEST saga: Implications for licensure and employment testing. The Bar Examiner, 68, 23–31.

Messick, S. (1989). Validity. In R. L. Linn (ed.). Educational Measurement, 3rd ed., 13–103. New York: Macmillan.

Moe, T. M. (2000). The two democratic purposes of public education. In L. M. McDonnell, P. M. Timpane, and R. Benjamin (eds.). Rediscovering the Democratic Purposes of Education, 127–147. Lawrence, Kan.: University Press of Kansas.

Nather, D. (June 30, 2001). Student-testing drive marks an attitude shift in Congress. CQ Weekly, 1560–1566.

National Alliance of Business. (2000). Improving Performance: Competition in American Public Education. http://www.nab.com/PDF/comp.pdf (last accessed May 13, 2002).

National Assessment of Educational Progress. (1987). Profiling American Education. No. 18-GIY. Princeton, N.J.: Educational Testing Service.

National Commission on Excellence in Education. (1983). A Nation at Risk. Washington, D.C.: U.S. Department of Education.

National Governors' Association. (1989). Results in Education: 1989. Washington, D.C.

National Research Council. (1998). Uncommon Measures: Equivalence and Linkage Among Educational Tests. M. J. Feuer, P. W. Holland, B. F. Green, M. W. Bertenthal, and F. C. Hemphill (eds.). Committee on Equivalency and Linkage of Educational Tests. Washington, D.C.: National Academy Press.

National Research Council, Committee on the Foundations of Assessment. (2001). Knowing What Students Know: The Science and Design of Educational Assessment. Washington, D.C.: National Academy Press.

Neufeld, S. (October 1, 2000). Backlash fermenting against school tests. San Jose Mercury News.

NPR Online. (1999). National Public Radio/Kaiser Family Foundation/Kennedy School Education Survey. http://www.npr.org/programs/specials/poll/education/education.results.html (last accessed May 10, 2002).

Olson, L. (June 6, 2001). States turn to end-of-course tests to bolster high school curriculum. Education Week, 20(39), 1, 26–27.

Phillips, S. E. (1993). Legal Implications of High-Stakes Assessment: What States Should Know. Michigan State University, North Central Regional Educational Laboratory, Illinois.

Pipho, C. (1985). Tracking the reforms, part 5: Testing—can it measure the success of the reform movement? Education Week, 4(35), 19.

Popham, W. J. (1987). The merits of measurement-driven instruction. Phi Delta Kappan, 68, 679–682.

Popham, W. J. (1992). A tale of two test-specification strategies. Educational Measurement: Issues and Practice, 11(2), 16–17, 22.

Popham, W. J., K. L. Cruse, S. C. Rankin, P. D. Sandifer, and P. L. Williams. (May 1985). Measurement-driven instruction: It's on the road. Phi Delta Kappan, 66(9), 628–634.

Public Agenda. (2000). Survey Finds Little Sign of Backlash Against Academic Standards or Standardized Tests. New York. http://www.publicagenda.org/aboutpa/pdf/standards-backlash.pdf (last accessed May 13, 2002).

Resnick, D. (1982). History of educational testing. In A. K. Wigdor and W. R. Garner (eds.). Ability Testing: Uses, Consequences, and Controversies, Part II. Washington, D.C.: National Academy Press, 173–194.

Rock, D. A., R. E. Bennett, and B. A. Kaplan. (1987). Internal construct validity of a college admissions test across handicapped and nonhandicapped groups. Educational and Psychological Measurement, 47, 193–205.

Roeber, E. (February 10, 1988). A history of large-scale testing activities at the state level. Paper presented at the Indiana Governor's Symposium on ISTEP. Madison, Ind.

Rogosa, D. R. (1999). Accuracy of Individual Scores Expressed as Percentile Ranks: Classical Test Theory Calculations. CSE Technical Report 509. Los Angeles: National Center for Research on Evaluation, Standards, and Student Testing.

Romberg, T. A., E. A. Zarinia, and S. R. Williams. (1989). The Influence of Mandated Testing on Mathematics Instruction: Grade 8 Teachers' Perceptions. Madison, Wis.: National Center for Research in Mathematical Science Education, University of Wisconsin–Madison.

Rose, L. C., and A. M. Gallup. (2000). The 32nd annual Phi Delta Kappa/Gallup poll of the public's attitudes toward the public schools. Phi Delta Kappan, 82(1), 41–57.

Russakoff, D. (February 10, 2001). A tough question for the testers. Washington Post.

Sanders, W. L., and S. P. Horn. (1998). Research findings from the Tennessee Value-Added Assessment System (TVAAS) database: Implications for educational evaluation and research. Journal of Personnel Evaluation in Education, 12, 247–256.

Schrag, P. (August 2000). High stakes are for tomatoes. The Atlantic Monthly, 286(2), 19–21.

Shavelson, R. J., G. P. Baxter, and X. Gao. (1993). Sampling variability of performance assessments. Journal of Educational Measurement, 30, 215–232.

Shavelson, R. J., and N. M. Webb. (1991). Generalizability Theory: A Primer. Newbury Park, Calif.: Sage.

Shepard, L. A. (1991). Will National Tests Improve Student Learning? CSE Technical Report 342. Los Angeles: National Center for Research on Evaluation, Standards, and Student Testing.

Shepard, L. A., and K. C. Dougherty. (1991). Effects of high-stakes testing on instruction. Paper presented at the annual meeting of the American Educational Research Association and the National Council on Measurement in Education, Chicago.

Smith, M. L. (1994). Old and New Beliefs About Measurement-Driven Instruction: "The More Things Change, the More They Stay the Same." CSE Technical Report 373. Los Angeles: National Center for Research on Evaluation, Standards, and Student Testing.

Smith, M. L. (1997). Reforming Schools by Reforming Assessment: Consequences of the Arizona Student Assessment Program (ASAP): Equity and Teacher Capacity Building. CSE Technical Report 425. Los Angeles: National Center for Research on Evaluation, Standards, and Student Testing.

Smith, M. L., C. Edelsky, K. Draper, C. Rottenberg, and M. Cherland. (1991). The Role of Testing in Elementary Schools. CSE Technical Report 321. Los Angeles: National Center for Research on Evaluation, Standards, and Student Testing.

Smith, M., and J. O'Day. (1991). Systemic school reform. In S. H. Fuhrman and B. Malen (eds.). The Politics of Curriculum and Testing, 233–268. Bristol, Pa.: Falmer Press.

Smith, M. L., and C. Rottenberg. (1991). Unintended consequences of external testing in elementary schools. Educational Measurement, Issues and Practice, 10(4), 7–11.

Solano-Flores, G., J. Jovanovic, R. J. Shavelson, and M. Bachman. (1999). On the development and evaluation of a shell for generating science performance assessments. International Journal of Science Education, 21(3), 293–315.

Stecher, B. M., and S. I. Barron. (1999). Quadrennial Milepost Accountability Testing in Kentucky. CSE Technical Report 505. Los Angeles: National Center for Research on Evaluation, Standards, and Student Testing.

Stecher, B. M., S. I. Barron, T. Chun, and K. Ross. (2000a). The Effects of the Washington State Education Reform on Schools and Classrooms. CSE Technical Report 525. Los Angeles: National Center for Research on Evaluation, Standards, and Student Testing.

Stecher, B. M., S. I. Barron, T. Kaganoff, and J. Goodwin. (1998). The Effects of Standards-Based Assessment on Classroom Practices: Results of the 1996–97 RAND Survey of Kentucky Teachers of Mathematics and Writing. CSE Technical Report 482. Los Angeles: National Center for Research on Evaluation, Standards, and Student Testing.

Stecher, B. M., and T. Chun. (2001). School and Classroom Practices During Two Years of Education Reform in Washington State. CSE Technical Report 550. Los Angeles: National Center for Research on Evaluation, Standards, and Student Testing.

Stecher, B. M., and S. P. Klein. (1997). The cost of science performance assessments in large-scale testing programs. Educational Evaluation and Policy Analysis, 19, 1–14.

Stecher, B. M., S. P. Klein, G. Solano-Flores, D. McCaffrey, A. Robyn, R. J. Shavelson, and E. H. Haertel. (2000b). The effect of content, format, and inquiry level on science performance assessment scores. Applied Measurement in Education, 13(2), 139–160.

Stecher, B. M., and K. J. Mitchell. (1995). Portfolio Driven Reform; Vermont Teachers' Understanding of Mathematical Problem Solving. CSE Technical Report 400. Los Angeles: National Center for Research on Evaluation, Standards, and Student Testing.

Stocking, M., T. Jirele, C. Lewis, and L. Swanson. (1998). Moderating possible irrelevant multiple mean score differences on a test of mathematical reasoning. Journal of Educational Measurement, 35, 1–24.

Stodolsky, S. S. (1998). The Subject Matters: Classroom Activity in Math and Social Studies. Chicago: University of Chicago Press.

Supovitz, J. A., and R. T. Brennan. (1997). Mirror, mirror on the wall, which is the fairest test of all? An examination of the equitability of portfolio assessment relative to standardized tests. Harvard Educational Review, 67, 472–503.

Teachers vote to let parents decide on tests. (July 8, 2001). New York Times, A15.

Thurlow, M. L., J. E. Ysseldyke, and B. Silverstein. (1993). Testing Accommodations for Students with Disabilities: A Review of the Literature. Synthesis Report 4. Minneapolis: National Center on Educational Outcomes, University of Minnesota.

Tippets, E., and H. Michaels. (1997). Factor structure invariance of accommodated and non-accommodated performance assessments. Paper presented at Annual Meeting of the National Council on Measurement in Education. Chicago.

Toch, T. (January 11, 1984). E.D. issues study ranking states on education. Education Week. http://www.edweek.org/ew/ewstory.cfm?slug=05280012.h03&keywords=Toch (last accessed May 13, 2002).

Valencia, R. R., and R. J. Rankin. (1985). Evidence of context bias on the McCarthy Scales with Mexican-American children: Implications for test translation and nonbiased assessment. Journal of Educational Psychology, 77(2), 197–207.

Wainer, H., and D. Thissen. (1993). Combining multiple-choice and constructed response test scores: Toward a Marxist theory of test construction. Applied Measurement in Education, 6, 103–118.

Washington Post. (2000). Washington Post/Kaiser Family Foundation/Harvard University. Issues I: Education. http://www.washingtonpost.com/wp-srv/politics/polls/vault/stories/data061800.htm (last accessed May 10, 2002).

Wilgoren, J. (July 17, 2001). School test plan comes under fire by state officials. New York Times, A1, A16.

Willingham, W. W., and N. S. Cole. (1997). Gender and Fair Assessment. Mahwah, N.J.: Erlbaum.

Wilson, K. (1980). The performance of minority students beyond the freshman year: Testing the "late bloomer" hypothesis in one state university setting. Research in Higher Education, 13(1), 23–47.

Wolf, S. A., H. Borko, M. C. McIver, and R. Elliott. (1999). "No Excuses": School Reform Efforts in Exemplary Schools of Kentucky. CSE Technical Report 514. Los Angeles: National Center for Research on Evaluation, Standards, and Student Testing.

Wolf, S. A., and M. C. McIver. (1999). When process becomes policy. Phi Delta Kappan, 80(5), 401–406.

Yen, W. M., and S. Ferrara. (1997). The Maryland School Performance Assessment Program: Performance assessment with psychometric quality suitable for high stakes usage. Educational and Psychological Measurement, 57(1), 60–84.

Zernike, K. (May 4, 2001). Suburban mothers succeed in their boycott of an 8th-grade test. New York Times, A19.

Ziebarth, T. (August 2000). Rewards and Sanctions for School Districts and Schools. Denver: Education Commission of the States.

Laura Hamilton
RAND Education

Stephen Klein
RAND Education

Daniel Koretz
Harvard University

Vi-Nhuan Le
RAND Education

Lorraine McDonnell
University of California, Santa Barbara

Brian Stecher
RAND Education